SOMERSET
DOG FRIENDLY
PUB WALKS

PAUL BOOBYER

COUNTRYSIDE BOOKS
NEWBURY BERKSHIRE

First published 2019
© 2019 Paul Boobyer

COUNTRYSIDE BOOKS
3 Catherine Road
Newbury, Berkshire

To view our complete range of books please visit us at
www.countrysidebooks.co.uk

ISBN 978 1 84674 384 9

All materials used in the manufacture of this book carry FSC certification

Produced by The Letterworks Ltd., Reading
Designed and Typeset by KT Designs, St Helens
Printed by Holywell Press, Oxford

Contents

Walk

INTRODUCTION

Many people will agree that combining a country walk with their dog and a visit to a decent, dog friendly pub is a perfect way to spend a day. This book will enable you to do just that! You may wonder what makes a dog friendly pub walk different from any other walk. The answer will be apparent to anyone who owns a dog and has planned a journey from a pub using a walking guide not aimed at dog owners. In attempting the walks in such guides, the dog owner will encounter numerous stiles that cannot be surmounted by most dogs, and which lack liftable boards designed to let dogs through. Occasionally Ordnance Survey maps have limitations for planning walks: the dashed lines on the maps indicate public rights of way, but the reality is that some of these paths are not maintained and are no longer in use, or hedges thick with bramble have grown over stiles, particularly in the Somerset Levels.

This book has been carefully planned to take these factors into account. In fact, in all the twenty walks in this book, there are only three stiles which require a dog to be lifted over them (two stiles on Walk 13 and one on Walk 15), and all the walks are on well-maintained routes, with minimal walking on quiet minor roads and sections where you can let your dog off the lead. That said, it has not been possible to produce a guide to dog friendly pub walks in Somerset without some walks through fields where livestock might be present. But as far as possible, the routes have been designed to avoid livestock, particularly cows, and information on where livestock may be present is included in each walk description. Most walks are circuits but a few are linear. Although you may find yourself retracing your outward route, the change of perspective should enable you to enjoy the route in both directions.

Of course, one of the best features of this guide is that all the walks start and finish at a decent dog friendly pub, most of which are well-known for the quality of the food they serve. Our national affection for dogs is particularly apparent in the pub culture of Britain, where a dog is often a conversation-starter between strangers, and we are fortunate that so many pubs in Somerset welcome dogs. This guide provides information on the number of real ales and ciders the pub has to offer, as well as historical information about the walk, location and pub.

One of the stars of this book is Indy, an Italian Spinone with an amiable personality and an innate and unrelenting urge to sniff everything – she is after all, a gundog. Spinones are an ancient breed renowned for their good nature and I am indebted to Indy's owners, the Snowshill family, for entrusting me with this four-legged companion for some very memorable adventures in Somerset. I hope this book enables you to enjoy visiting some fantastic pubs and exploring Somerset's enchanting countryside with your four-legged friends as much as I did.

Paul Boobyer

The challenge level attributed to each walk is rated according to difficulty, with 1 being the easiest and 4 being the most challenging:

Level 1: Almost entirely flat or involving very gentle inclines and well-maintained footpaths.

Level 2: Gentle inclines with some slightly steeper sections. Footpaths are generally well-maintained.

Level 3: Some steep inclines, but overall not beyond the ability of someone with a moderate level of fitness. Footpaths may be less maintained.

Level 4: Steep inclines that will be uncomfortable for walkers with less than a moderate level of fitness. Footpaths may be less maintained.

PUBLISHER'S NOTE

We hope that you and your dog obtain considerable enjoyment from this book; great care has been taken in its preparation. In order to assist in navigation to the start point of the walk, we have included the nearest postcode, however, a postcode cannot always deliver you to a precise starting point, especially in rural areas. Although at the time of publication all routes followed public rights of way or permitted paths, diversion orders can be made and permissions withdrawn.

We cannot, of course, be held responsible for such diversion orders or any inaccuracies in the text which result from these or any other changes to the routes, nor any damage which might result from walkers trespassing on private property. We are anxious, though, that all the details covering the walks are kept up to date, and would therefore welcome information from readers which would be relevant to future editions.

The simple sketch maps that accompany the walks in this book are based on notes made by the author whilst surveying the routes on the ground. They are designed to show you how to reach the start and to point out the main features of the overall circuit, and they contain a progression of numbers that relate to the paragraphs of the text.

However, for the benefit of a proper map, we do recommend that you purchase the relevant Ordnance Survey sheet covering your walk – details of the relevant sheet are with each walk.

ADVICE FOR DOG WALKERS

'The countryside is a great place to exercise dogs, but it is every owner's duty to make sure their dog is not a danger or nuisance to farm animals, wildlife or other people.' *(Taken from the Government's 'Code for the Public'. The full code is available on the Government's Countryside Access website: www.countrysideaccess.gov.uk.)*

Please also note the following:

- Large areas of Somerset, including moorland and woodland, are home to ground-nesting birds that should remain undisturbed through the nesting season (March to July inclusive). Pheasants are reared in fenced pens and released in their hundreds into woodlands and onto moorlands around September, particularly on the Quantocks and Exmoor. Please observe any notices in such areas which typically will advise that dogs should be kept on a lead.
- Sheep and lambs will generally move away from dogs. Unfortunately, some dogs find that fun and give chase. This stresses the animals and can cause ewes to abort (January to March is lambing time) and livestock owners are entitled to shoot dogs worrying livestock. You may see notices that dogs worrying sheep will be shot.
- Cattle are generally inquisitive and will move towards dogs, forming a semi-circle as they approach you. They are not generally harmful but a cow who considers her calf to be threatened may behave aggressively. In such cases, drop the dog's lead. The cow will most likely chase the dog and not you. A dog may be able to outrun a charging cow, but it is likely that you won't.

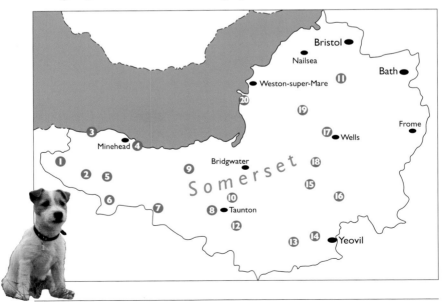

- There are lots of wild ponies in Somerset, particularly on the Quantock Hills and Exmoor. They are not generally bothered by dogs or people and generally move away if approached. That said, it is best if you keep a respectful distance from them, especially if you are with a dog.
- Tick populations are increasing, particularly in the Quantock Hills and Exmoor, where sheep, deer and pheasants roam freely. Take precautions against Lyme disease, particularly in these areas.

Ticks and Lyme Disease

Ticks mainly feed off sheep, deer and pheasants until fully bloated and then drop off. They tend to cling to the edge of scrub plants, particularly bracken. Dogs running through bracken and undergrowth or lying down on open moorland are liable to pick up ticks. Both dogs and humans are an attractive food source for ticks and you don't usually feel the bite. They can carry Lyme disease, which should always be treated by a doctor. However, you can help to avoid tick bites by taking the following advice:

Wear long trousers, tucked into socks, and long-sleeved shirts – even in hot weather.

Light-coloured clothing makes the ticks easier to spot. Ticks are black or dark brown in colour.

Always check yourself and your dog at the end of a walk. The ticks are easy to brush off if they haven't attached themselves.

Insect repellents for dogs may help.

If a tick has attached itself, it can generally be removed with tweezers. Place the tweezers around the tick, as close as you can possibly get to the skin. Don't twist or jerk the tick, just pull gently upwards, adding pressure until the tick lets go of the skin. Alternatively, tick removers may be bought at most Somerset vets.

The symptoms of Lyme disease are generally flu-like to begin with but can lead to serious complications if not treated.

1 SIMONSBATH
4.1 miles (6.6 km)

This pleasant jaunt on part of the Two Moors Way long-distance footpath follows the course of the River Barle to Cow Castle, a Scheduled Ancient Monument and site of a Bronze Age hillfort dating to around 800 BC – AD 100. The Barle is one of the two main rivers that originate on Exmoor (the other being the River Exe), which gives the moor its name. Well-behaved dogs can run free on most of this walk and there are several places providing easy access to the river for water-loving canines.

The hillfort site is surrounded by a rampart up to two metres high and has a single entrance eight metres wide on the eastern side. Within the enclosure are the remnants of at least four house platforms. From here you may spot red deer and wild Exmoor ponies grazing on the surrounding hillsides.

Along the way you pass the ruin of Wheal Eliza. This ruined mine was opened in 1845 (originally called Wheal Maria) and despite samples indicating metallic ore of 60%, no copper or iron was successfully extracted. The mine was consequently abandoned and allowed to flood in 1857.

> **How to get there:** The inn is located just east of the village of Simonsbath at the junction of the B3223 and the B3358.
> **Sat Nav TA24 7SH**.
> **Parking:** Ashcombe car park is 250 metres from the Exmoor Forest Inn, accessed via a small lane next to the pub. There is also parking outside the pub, subject to the landlord's discretion.
> **OS Map:** Explorer OL9 Exmoor/Landranger 180 Barnstaple & Ilfracombe. **Grid ref:** SS773392.

THE PUB **EXMOOR FOREST INN** welcomes dogs in the bar areas and in some of the hotel accommodation and can lend your undoubtedly contented canine items such as a dog towel and food bowl during your stay.

The building resembles a Bavarian alpine hotel from the outside but inside it is quintessentially British. It has a bar area divided into three sections, as well as a dining area and a beer garden, and is well-known locally for its high-end cuisine, including vegetarian dishes. There is a cosy open fire to enjoy during the colder months and the bar serves a choice of three local real ales and two West Country ciders, as well as coffee and cream teas. Closed on Monday in winter (Oct–Mar).

🌐 exmoorforestinn.co.uk ☎ 01643 831341

Terrain: Mostly flat on well-made paths, with only a few gentle slopes in a picturesque landscape characterised by shallow, meandering grass-covered valleys.
Challenge level: 1.
Road walking: None.
Livestock: Possibility of sheep from halfway between points 1 and 2.
Stiles: None.
Nearest vet: Dulverton Veterinary Practice, Dulverton TA22 9HJ.
☎ 01398 323285.

The Walk

1 Cross the B3223 outside the Exmoor Forest Inn and bear right on the footpath opposite the pub, ignoring the waymarked footpath bearing off to

the left towards the Picked Stones. The path is flanked by woodland but soon the tree cover ends and you find yourself in a landscape of small, shallow grassy valleys.

2 One mile (1.6 km) from the start of the walk you pass the ruins of Wheal Eliza. *There is hardly anything left at the site today, although a former wagon access route is visible on the south side of the Barle opposite the ruined mine building.*

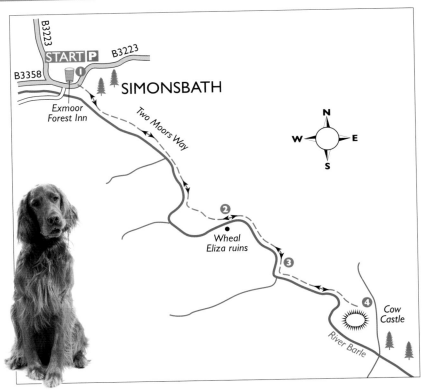

❸ At a junction of paths 620 metres after Wheal Eliza, continue straight ahead adjacent to the river and between overgrown beech hedges towards Cow Castle.

❹ At Cow Castle, 0.9 miles (1.5 km) after Wheal Eliza, you can scramble up the fort's steep slope to get a view of the surrounding valley and contemplate the lives people led here in the Bronze Age; then return the way you came for a refreshing drink at the Exmoor Forest Inn.

2 TARR STEPS
1.9 or 7.2 miles (3.1 or 11.6 km)

A visit to the historic 'clapper' bridge (derived from the Latin 'claperius', meaning 'pile of stones') at Tarr Steps and a refreshment at the rustically quaint Tarr Farm Inn is one of the must-do experiences on the lists of many visitors to Exmoor. The Inn receives coach-loads of tourists in summer so bear this in mind when planning a trip as parking is limited. If you plan on eating at the inn it is advised that you book in advance, especially during busier times.

The bridge at Tarr Steps is Grade I listed and a Scheduled Ancient Monument. It is at least of medieval origin but could date to the Bronze Age (there is some contention as to its actual age). However, the bridge has been reassembled several times since its construction, due to being damaged in floods.

The walk leads north on the eastern bank of the River Barle through ancient semi-natural woodland (a National Nature Reserve) and follows part of the Two Moors Way to Withypool. You could make the walk slightly shorter by crossing the river via some stepping stones just south of Withypool. The stones are stable and large, although some lie at sloping angles. When the river level is high after heavy rain or if you don't have confidence in your balance, it's best to continue to Withypool.

Well-behaved dogs can run leash-free between Tarr Farm Inn and the end of the woodland after point 2 (opposite North Batsom farm on OS maps). The Royal Oak Inn in Withypool may be open for refreshments but was closed for business when the author visited.

Terrain: The path takes you through a landscape of hedges, woodland copses and fields. There are some gentle inclines and declines, but overall the walk is relatively flat.
Challenge level: 2.
Road walking: 1.9 miles/3.1 km.
Livestock: Possibility of sheep or cattle after point 2.
Stiles: Two, both of which have dog boards next to them.
Nearest vet: Dulverton Veterinary Practice, Dulverton, TA22 9HJ.
☎ 01398 323285.

How to get there: The Tarr Farm Inn is located close to a ford on a lane just west of the hamlet of Liscombe.
Sat Nav TA22 9PY for pay-and-display car park.
Parking: There is a pay-and-display car park 350 metres north of Tarr Steps, on the only road leading to and from the inn, signposted from Liscombe. Parking at the inn is only permitted for B&B residents. Parking is also available in Withypool.
OS Map: Explorer OL9 Exmoor/Landranger 181 Minehead & Brendon Hills. **Grid ref:** SS872323.

THE PUB

THE TARR FARM INN is immensely popular and is known for the quality of its food (expect to pay high-end prices if dining here). There is a small bar which serves one regular ale and one changing ale, and a larger restaurant area. There are three log-burning stoves in the building and a cosy lounge for residents, replete with dark leather sofas and an open fire. Dogs are permitted in the bar area and residents' lounge but not in the dining room.

The pub also serves as a tearoom and its cream teas are well received. If you fancy indulging in some of the West Country's finest cuisine, this riverside idyll with its slate-topped tables overlooked by chattering magpies and lulled by leaves whispering on a summer breeze is a perfect place to do so.
⊕ tarrfarm.co.uk ☎ 01643 851507

The Walk

. . . .

❶ From the car park, turn left and walk 350 metres to the Tarr Farm Inn. From here, head upriver on the footpath next to the River Barle's east bank and continue through mature deciduous woodland to a footbridge that crosses the river.

SOMERSET – Dog Friendly Pub Walks

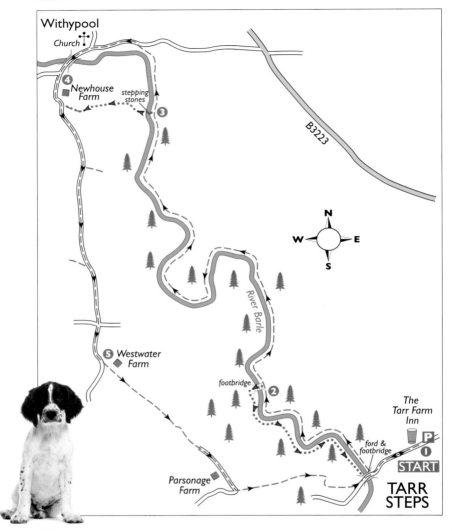

2 If you fancy a shorter walk of 1.9 miles (3.1 km), cross the footbridge and turn left when reaching the west bank of the river, then head downriver back to Tarr Steps. Otherwise, continue on the east bank of the river past the footbridge, heading upriver towards Withypool.

3 After around 2.2 miles (3.5 km) you will see some stepping stones on your left. You can cross the Barle here, knocking 1 mile (1.6 km) off the walk, or continue upriver on the same path towards Withypool, where you go over a couple of stiles (with dog gates next to them) before reaching a

public road. Turn left when joining the road to go through the village, passing a church, café (The Filling Station), village shop and public toilets. Cross the stone bridge over the Barle and continue on the road heading uphill out of the village.

4 Turn left at a gate and waymarker indicating Tarr Steps. Here you head onto a narrow lane (Worth Lane) just beyond some houses. Pass Newhouse Farm and continue for around 1.5 miles (2.3 km) to Westwater Farm.

5 Just after Westwater Farm, turn left onto the public footpath and follow it through fields for 1 mile (1.6 km) until reaching Parsonage Farm. Turn left when meeting an unmetalled lane near the farm entrance and follow it for 800 metres until reaching Tarr Steps. The Tarr Farm Inn is 100 metres beyond.

© Lorna Anness

© Lorna Anness

3 PORLOCK WEIR

5.3 miles (8.5 km)

This delightful excursion treats you to splendid views across the Bristol Channel to the south coast of Wales. There are also plenty of intriguing scents for your dog to follow in ancient woodland. The first half of the route requires some exertion due to steep coombes. Well-controlled dogs can run free between points 2 and 6, after which you return to Porlock Weir on quiet, minor roads.

Leaving the picturesque harbour of Porlock Weir, the path ascends between fields into woodland to pass the attractive Worthy Coombe Toll and continues through tunnels dug in the 19th century for nearby Worthy Manor. At the time the manor was owned by Ada Lovelace, who was a talented mathematician and is credited as being the first person to write an algorithm intended for the Analytical Engine, the world's first mechanical computing machine, produced in 1837. As such, Ada is sometimes regarded as the world's first computer programmer.

The path continues through woodland to St Beuno's Church (better known as Culbone Church), Britain's smallest complete church. The church is only ten and a half metres long with a congregation capacity of just 33. Parts of the building date from Saxon times (i.e. pre-Norman Conquest in 1066). Take time to savour the peaceful atmosphere in the churchyard, where a bench makes a good place for a packed lunch.

SOMERSET – Dog Friendly Pub Walks

After point 6 you pass Ash Farm, where the poet Samuel Taylor Coleridge wrote his esteemed but unfinished poem *Kubla Khan* in 1797. While not composing poetry, Coleridge spent a lot of time at Ash befuddled by opium, supplied by a doctor from Porlock.

How to get there: Porlock Weir is at the end of a minor road accessed from the nearby village of Porlock, which is just off the A39. The Ship Inn is opposite a large car park at the end of the road leading from Porlock.
Sat Nav TA24 8PB.
Parking: The only parking available at Porlock Weir is a pay-and-display car park opposite the Ship Inn. Due to limited parking it is advised that you arrive by mid-morning in the busy summer months.
OS Map: Explorer OL9 Exmoor/Landranger 181 Minehead & Brendon Hills. **Grid ref:** SS864477.

Terrain: The route is graded as challenge level 4 due to the steep slopes. However, the reward for your effort is great views and being enclosed by ancient forest for about half of the walk, along a section of the South West Coast Path. The paths are well-maintained.
Challenge level: 4.
Road walking: 2 miles/3.2 km.
Livestock: None.
Stiles: None.
Nearest vet: White Lodge Veterinary Clinic, Minehead, TA24 5EB. ☎ 01643 703649 or Glenmore House Veterinary Surgery, Minehead, TA24 5BH. ☎ 01643 703175.

THE PUB

THE SHIP INN is also known as the Bottom Ship to avoid confusion with another Ship Inn in neighbouring Porlock. The building is thatched with flagstone floors and has been the social hub in Porlock Weir for over 400 years. The pub has a small bar area, a larger dining area, and a beer garden with outdoor seating. Dogs are welcome in the bar and outdoor areas, and

© Lorna Anness

in the B&B accommodation. The bar serves three regular ales, two changing ales, and two West Country ciders. You can luxuriate in front of an open fire in the colder months.

A beer festival (Weirfest) is hosted by the Ship Inn during the first week of July, with up to 50 ales and ciders available. It's best to check the dates of the festival if you plan on walking then as car access is prohibited during the festival.

🌐 shipinnporlockweir.co.uk ☎ 01643 863288

© Lorna Anness

The Walk

• •

❶ From the northern side of the Ship Inn (i.e. turning left on leaving the pub), follow the waymarked South West Coast Path leading uphill behind the Anchor Hotel, to a path passing between fields and ascending into woodland.

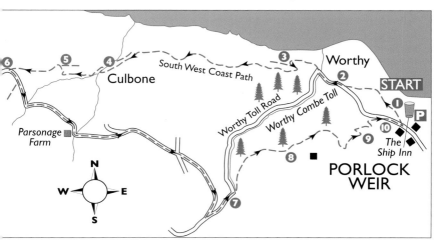

© Lorna Anness

2 The path joins a minor asphalt road at the hamlet of Worthy. Head uphill on the road, following the South West Coast Path and skirting Worthy Coombe Toll, an attractive gate lodge guarding a private road.

3 The path becomes steeper and passes through tunnels dug to provide Worthy Manor with access to a private beach nearby. Keep following the South West Coast Path waymarkers to Culbone Church, ignoring the unwaymarked paths.

4 After visiting Culbone Church exit the churchyard through a small gate on a public right of way to Silcombe Farm B&B (ignore the notice stating no path to Porlock Weir). This streamside path takes you uphill under an arch next to Culbone Lodge.

5 At a junction of paths, you re-join the South West Coast Path and turn left, heading towards the waymarked Silcombe Farm B&B and Lynmouth. Here you leave the woodland to enter a landscape of fields and small copses.

6 When meeting a minor road, turn left and follow the waymarker towards Parsonage Farm. On a clear day you will see the south coast of Wales across the Bristol Channel. At the crossroads 1.1 miles (1.7 km) after joining the minor road, keep going straight ahead on the signposted road towards Porlock Weir.

7 When reaching the top of Worthy Toll Road, turn right onto a track waymarked as the Coleridge Way, heading into woodland dominated by sessile oak and holly. Don't walk down the private toll road.

8 Turn left at a waymarker indicating a public bridleway to Porlock Weir. Keep to this wider track and avoid narrow tracks that branch off from it a little further down the hill.

9 Turn left at another bridleway towards Porlock Weir, waymarked as the Coleridge Way.

© Lorna Anness

10 After passing behind some houses, the path joins an asphalt road. Here you turn right, heading downhill for 170 metres, and then turn left onto another road to descend to the Ship Inn.

© Lorna Anness

4 DUNSTER
2.9 miles (4.7 km)

This scenic hike is a great work-out for you and your dog and the expansive views from Grabbist Hill make the effort worthwhile. Well-behaved dogs can explore and run leash-free from just after point 2 until point 8.

From Dunster the route ascends and skirts the northern flank of Grabbist Hill, then continues to the hill's rounded ridge where you join part of the Macmillan Way West, a long-distance footpath. When in bloom, the heather-clad summit of Grabbist Hill looks stunning and provided the inspiration for a verse in the hymn *All Things Bright and Beautiful*, written in 1848. After passing the summit, you head steeply downhill back to Dunster for a drink in one of Exmoor's most elegant pubs.

Dunster village was established to service Dunster Castle, built by the Normans in 1096 as part of their subjugation of Somerset. For centuries the village was an important centre of wool and cloth production and trade. However, by the early 18th century trade decreased and the fortunes of the village declined until the beginnings of early tourism in the late 18th century. Dunster remains a popular destination and is often regarded as one of the prettiest villages on Exmoor due to its medieval aspect. A walk along the High Street is recommended.

Terrain: The route mostly traverses open hillsides on well-maintained and waymarked paths. There are some relatively steep sections, but this walk is fine for anyone with a moderate level of fitness.
Challenge level: 3.
Road walking: 237 metres.
Livestock: None.
Stiles: None.
Nearest vet: White Lodge Veterinary Clinic, Minehead, TA24 5EB. ☎ 01643 703649 or Glenmore House Veterinary Surgery, Minehead, TA24 5BH. ☎ 01643 703175.

How to get there: From the A39, head south on the A396 at a junction 0.8 miles (1.3 km) south of Minehead. Dunster is 360 metres south from that junction. The Luttrell Arms Hotel is at the northern end of the High Street.
Sat Nav TA24 6AS.
Parking: There is a pay-and-display car park just to the north of the Luttrell Arms Hotel on the A396, which leads into Dunster High Street. On-street parking in Dunster is limited in the busy summer months.
OS Map: Explorer OL9 Exmoor/Landranger 181 Minehead & Brendon Hills. **Grid ref:** SS992439.

THE PUB

THE LUTTRELL ARMS HOTEL is a Grade II listed building and one of Exmoor's grandest pubs. The bar serves two regular ales, two changing ales and one West Country cider, and its restaurant is known for the quality of its food. There is also a pleasant courtyard and a small snug opposite the bar entrance. Dogs are allowed in the bar, snug and courtyard areas.

It is worth visiting the hotel if only to see the building, which dates from at least 1443, when it was three individual houses. Later it became a guesthouse for abbots at Cleeve Abbey, one of the best-preserved medieval monasteries in England, 4.5 miles (7.3 km) away just outside Washford. The building has been tastefully altered over the years and still retains some antique features, including the oldest window glass in Somerset and 16th-century plasterwork on the lounge ceiling.

The hotel is named after the Luttrell family who owned Dunster Castle from the 14th–20th centuries.
⊕ luttrellarms.co.uk
☎ 01643 821555

The Walk

. . . .

1 From the Luttrell Arms, cross the High Street and head uphill (north) on a narrow asphalt lane to meet a lane called The Ball. Here you turn left, passing cottages and heading uphill to a gate next to a thatched cottage (Northanger), and continue straight ahead on a grassy lane next to Dunster Orchard.

2 At the Butter Cross – a medieval cross that was once in the village centre (the top part of the cross is now missing), turn left onto St Georges Street and continue downhill for 81 metres to Hanger's Way, a narrow lane on your right. Here you follow a waymarker indicating Grabbist Hill, heading uphill on a bridleway in the direction of Ellicombe, waymarked a little further ahead.

3 At a fork in the track bear left to go up a steep slope indicated by a public bridleway waymarker.

4 Turn right at a junction of bridleways, heading downhill towards Minehead, and pass through another junction of bridleways where you continue straight ahead towards Alcombe.

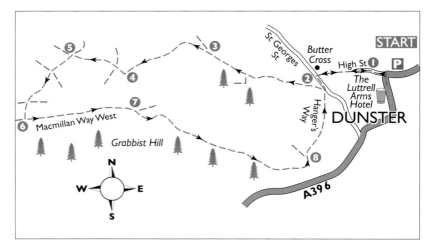

5 At an unwaymarked crossroads fork left onto a lesser-used path and continue uphill. At the next path junction 150 metres ahead, keep going straight ahead, following a blue waymarker on a wooden post.

6 Bear left onto a wide bridleway (part of the Macmillan Way West) heading downhill.

7 At a junction marked by a National Trust sign, continue straight ahead to go downhill on a track traversing a steep wooded hillside.

8 At the junction bear left towards Dunster. Here you leave the woodland and continue on a minor road passing allotments, then continue straight ahead behind a bench onto a narrow asphalt path leading to Hanger's Way. At the end of Hanger's Way turn left onto St Georges Street and head back to Dunster via the Butter Cross.

© Lorna Anness

5 WINSFORD
5.1 miles (8.2 km)

This walk is a real adventure incorporating woodland, moorland, an ancient lane and a fascinating stone commemorating a descendant of a Celtic warrior. Your dog can be let off the lead from point 3. However, if your pooch has sheep-worrying tendencies, it may need to be put on the leash again if sheep are present after point 6, where the path enters moorland.

The walk starts by heading uphill out of Winsford on Yellowcombe Lane, an ancient route to Winsford Hill cut deep into the ground from years of use and is overarched by a verdant canopy, including an abundance of holly. After leaving the lane, you continue steeply uphill through woodland and over moorland to the Caratacus Stone.

The Caratacus Stone dates to the 6th century AD and commemorates a descendent of the 1st-century chieftain Caratacus, who led the *Catuvellauni*, a Celtic tribe from what is now south-east England. The *Catuvellauni* resisted the Roman conquest of Britain for ten years until Caratacus was captured. Surprisingly, he was spared execution and was freed to live in Rome with his family. The stone is inscribed in Latin, but due to weathering it is difficult to see the letters. After admiring the Stone, you continue over moorland to join the route you walked earlier and head back to Winsford.

Terrain: The route ascends from points 1 to 7, with some steep sections. The paths are mostly well-maintained, although you may find some bracken and brambles brushing your legs around point 5. The moorland area between points 6 and 8, shown on OS maps as 'The Allotment', is relatively level.
Challenge level: 3.
Road walking: 225 metres.
Livestock: Possibly partridges between points 2 and 3 and possibility of sheep after point 6.
Stiles: 1 with no dog board. Option to use a gate instead, via a shallow ford.
Nearest vet: Dulverton Veterinary Practice, Dulverton, TA22 9HJ.
☎ 01398 323285.

How to get there: Winsford is 1.4 miles (2.2 km) from the A396, running between Tiverton and Minehead. The Royal Oak is on Halse Lane, about 70 metres from the village centre.
Sat Nav TA24 7JE.
Parking: The Royal Oak has a small car park, with parking at the landlord's discretion. On-street parking in Winsford is limited.
OS Map: Explorer OL9 Exmoor/Landranger 181 Minehead & Brendon Hills. **Grid ref:** SS905348.

THE PUB **THE ROYAL OAK EXMOOR** dates from the 12th century and was originally a farmhouse. It is now a popular pub and small, cosy hotel which has won several awards for its food. There is a small bar with an open fire and a larger dining area. The bar serves three regular ales (two in winter) and one cider. Dogs are permitted in the bar and in some of the hotel accommodation.
⊕ royaloakexmoor.co.uk ☎ 01643 851455

Winsford (5)

The Walk

1 When leaving the Royal Oak, turn left and head up the steep Halse Lane past some roadside cottages.

2 After 185 metres, turn left onto the bridleway (Yellowcombe Lane) at a waymarker indicating Dulverton, Tarr Steps and Winsford Hill. The path continues uphill until levelling out, then heads gently downhill. Signs here request dogs on leads as there are partridge keeps near the path.

3 Cross the stream via a stile and footbridge, or alternatively via a ford

© Lorna Anness

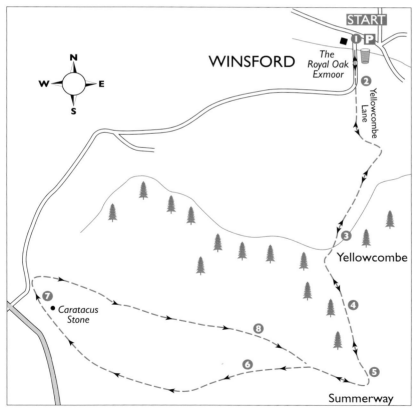

and gate, and continue through conifer woodland, passing a waymarker indicating 'Bridleway to Summerway'. Turn right when meeting a T-junction and keep going towards Summerway, indicated by a waymarker.

© Lorna Anness

4 You now join an unmetalled woodland track heading uphill. Shortly after, the route swings to the right onto a steep, narrow bridleway which emerges onto another unmetalled track.

5 Cross the track and head uphill on the path opposite to go through a gate where you turn right, heading towards the waymarked Tarr Steps and Spire Cross. Follow the field edge, keeping the fence to your right. Don't go through either of the gates in the corner of the field. Continue through two gates and past a waymarker indicating Winsford Hill along an unmetalled track.

6 Bear right at the waymarker indicating Spire X, keeping the fence and hedge of young beech to your right. The landscape opens to a grassy moorland with patches of heather and expansive views. Follow the fence on your right until you come to the Caratacus Stone.

7 From the Caratacus Stone, continue on the track keeping the hedge to your right, and then go through a gate and follow the waymarked route towards Winsford via Yellowcombe, Bridgetown and Summerway. The route is the more obvious of the two routes leading from the gate and stays on the higher ground.

8 When you come to a waymarker, keep going straight ahead towards Week Lane and re-join the route you walked earlier, to head back to Winsford.

© Lorna Anness

6 DULVERTON
2.3 miles (3.7 km)

If you like woodland walks, this pleasant circuit is a real gem. Well-controlled dogs can enjoy the numerous critter scent trails and water-loving canines can take a dip in the River Barle. Most of the woodland is a Site of Special Scientific Interest which contains rare lichens and is important habitat for woodland bird species such as the pied flycatcher. There is also the option of a short detour to the site of Oldberry Castle, a Scheduled Ancient Monument.

After leaving the Bridge Inn, you cross the River Barle and head uphill to enter Burridge Wood, where you follow the Exe Valley Way adjacent to the Barle. The walk then ascends and doubles back on itself to pass below Oldberry Castle, the site of one of three Iron Age hillforts that guarded a strategic position at a crossing point of the River Barle, where several thoroughfares converged. Turning right at a track heading uphill at point 5 will take you to the fort site. From point 5 the path then descends to re-join the route walked earlier and heads back over the bridge at Dulverton. Nestled deep in a wooded valley, the village is extremely picturesque and has a long history as a trading hub, with the woollen trade being of major importance until the early 18th century.

How to get there: Dulverton is 1.4 miles (2.2 km) west of the A396 (running between Taunton and Minehead) on the B3222. The Bridge Inn is at the bottom of Bridge Street.
Sat Nav TA22 9HJ for the pub or **TA22 9HZ** for public car park.
Parking: There are about eight car spaces just next to the bridge

> **Terrain:** After the initial ascent just after Barle Bridge, the way is almost totally flat until you reach a steep but short section where you ascend to double back on yourself. The path levels briefly before descending to Dulverton. The paths are well maintained.
> **Challenge level:** 2.
> **Road walking:** 345 metres.
> **Livestock:** None.
> **Stiles:** None.
> **Nearest vet:** Dulverton Veterinary Practice, Dulverton TH22 9HJ.
> ☎ 01398 323285.

opposite the Bridge Inn, with parking at the landlord's discretion. A large pay-and-display car park is located just behind the police station. To get there from the Bridge Inn, head along Kemps Way and follow the road as it swings round behind the police station.
OS Map: Explorer OL9 Exmoor/Explorer 114 Exeter & The Exe Valley/ Landranger 181 Minehead & Brendon Hills.
Grid ref: SS912278.

THE PUB

THE BRIDGE INN dates from 1845 and has gained commendations for its food by both the *Telegraph* and the *Guardian*. Your pooch won't miss out on culinary treats though, as dog biscuits are available at the bar, which serves one regular ale, three changing ales (less in winter) and a West Country cider. There are also some unusual imported bottled beers and a selection of 20 gins. There is an open fire to enjoy in the cooler months and on a warm day you can enjoy a drink or meal on one of the two terraces. The pub hosts an annual beer festival over the Whitsun holiday, which coincides with the local folk festival.
⊕ thebridgeinndulverton.com
☎ 01398 324130

© Lorna Anness

The Walk

. . . .

1 Cross the Barle Bridge, which has medieval origins, and turn right at Oldberry Lane on the other side, heading towards Burridge Wood as indicated by a waymarker, and continue for 245 metres to a junction of lanes.

2 Bear right at the junction, following the waymarker for Kennel Farm and passing Horner Cottage to continue on a footpath (part of the Exe Valley Way). About 100 metres after Horner Cottage keep going straight ahead on the path adjacent to the River Barle; don't turn left on the path going uphill, which is part of the return route. Continue next to the river for 0.7 miles (1.1 km) until the path starts to ascend and you meet a junction of two paths.

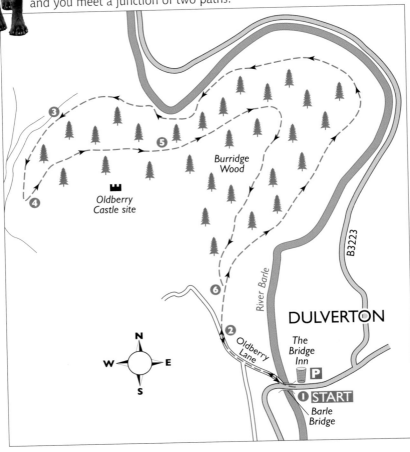

3 Turn left at the junction, waymarked as Middle Path, heading uphill.

4 Turn left at the second Middle Path waymarker to continue through pleasant woodland abundant with lichen-covered trees.

5 If you want to visit the site of Oldberry Castle, where not much remains other than the fort's mound, turn right to go uphill on a narrow path waymarked for the castle. Otherwise, continue on Middle Path, which descends towards the Barle.

6 At the path junction, turn right to re-join the Exe Valley Way and retrace your route back to Dulverton.

7 WATERROW
3.8 miles (6.1 km)

This pleasant sojourn on the western edge of the Brendon Hills, an Area of Outstanding Natural Beauty, takes you through rolling farmland and on quiet lanes. From the Rock Inn you ascend the steep Bibors Hill before heading off through fields on tracks, to re-join a minor road leading back to the Rock Inn via Bibors Hill.

Beware, signs in some fields en route request you to have wormed your dog prior to entering, due to the potential of infecting livestock. Be prepared to keep your dog on a lead or under close control if livestock are present.

How to get there: The B3227 between Wiveliscombe and Bampton passes in front of the pub.
Sat Nav TA4 2AX.
Parking: There is a small car park opposite the pub on the northern side of the bridge carrying the B3227 over the River Tone, with parking at the landlord's discretion. On-street parking near the pub is limited.
OS Map: Explorer 128 Taunton & Blackdown Hills/Landranger 181 Minehead & Brendon Hills. **Grid ref:** ST051253.

THE PUB

THE ROCK INN is built on the banks of the River Tone, and dates back to the 1600s. Part of the building was a smithy until 1850, when it was converted to a coaching inn. It has been expanded and modified over the years and some of the underlying bedrock has been incorporated into the building in the bar area, hence the inn's name. The pink cottage opposite

was an inn until the Rock Inn was converted. Shops, workshops and a toll house were once clustered around the adjacent bridge but have since been demolished.

The Rock Inn prides itself on its good-quality meals. Its bar serves three local ales and two West Country ciders. Most of the pub is given over to diners and the bar area consists of just one table, but there is also a snug room and there are a couple of benches outside. Dogs are permitted in some of the accommodation and on leads in the bar and dining areas. Closed on Monday in summer and also on Tuesday in winter.

🌐 rockinnwaterrow.co.uk ☎ 01984 623293

Terrain: The route is undulating but with no significant slopes, except for a steep stretch of several hundred metres on Bibors Hill near the Rock Inn.
Challenge level: 2.
Road walking: 1.1 miles/1.8 km.
Livestock: Possibility of sheep and cows between points 3 and 10.
Stiles: None.
Nearest vet: Deane Vets, Wiveliscombe, TA4 2RE. ☎ 01984 624405.

The Walk

❶ Leaving the Rock Inn, turn left to head uphill on a minor road (not the B3227) and after 57 metres, turn left again onto a steep, tree-lined Bibors Hill, heading west. Follow this minor road for about 400 metres.

❷ Follow the waymarked path heading off the road to the right into woodland to emerge shortly after onto an open hillside and continue to a metal gate.

❸ After going through the gate, bear to the left around the rim of the steep field towards some agricultural buildings. Don't follow the steep path heading straight down the hill.

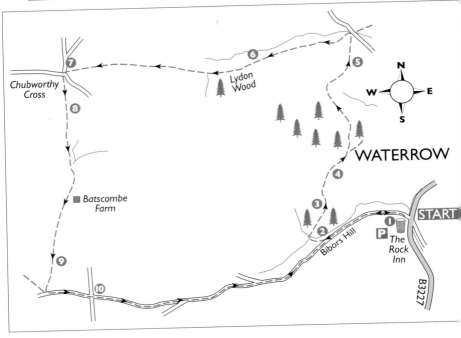

4 Go through a gate just below the agricultural buildings into an adjacent field where you follow a wooden ranch-style fence as it bears to the left. At the end of the fence pass through a gate and onto a track, turning right to head downhill for 620 metres until meeting a grassy track next to an oak tree.

5 Head down the grassy track, as indicated by a waymarker arrow, into young woodland beneath some telephone wires. At the bottom of the hill turn left and go through a gate, to turn immediately left, heading uphill on a track for 20 metres and through another gate, with a waymarker on its post, into a field. Follow the footpath through the field.

6 Pass through another gate into a small woodland (Lydon Wood) and then into another field after 200 metres.

7 Go through a gate at the field end to join a minor asphalt road at a junction (Chubworthy Cross) and head in the direction of Raddington and Skilgate (the road directly in front of you) for 12 metres, then turn left at the first field gate to enter the field. There is no waymarker here, but it is a public right of way. Keep close to the hedge on your left-hand side as you walk uphill through the field.

8 At the top corner of the field go through another gate and head onto the track heading downhill and leading into a small woodland. You then pass through the yard at Batscombe Farm and continue straight ahead on a farm track with a fence on your left and a hedge on your right. After 300 metres you arrive at a junction.

9 Leave the well-maintained path (which swings to the right) at the junction and keep going straight ahead through a gate into a field. At the bottom of the field go through a gate and turn left onto a track, turning left again after 20 metres onto a minor asphalt road.

10 The road meets a crossroads where you go straight across and follow the road for 1.1 miles (1.8 km) back to the Rock Inn.

8 BISHOP'S HULL
1.6 miles (2.6 km)

This tranquil circuit on the outskirts of Bishop's Hull takes you and your canine companion on a tour of Netherclay Community Woodland Nature Reserve. This 9.8-hectare reserve was established in 2004 and contains native deciduous tree species and an open grassy area. You can extend this walk by continuing straight ahead at point 6 for 800 metres (rather than turning right to head directly to point 7), turn right at the end of the second field, and then follow Norton Brook east to point 7, which would add 1.1 miles (1.7 km) to the walk.

The reserve is a great place for your dog to have a good run off the lead, and there are plenty of scent trails to keep it alert. For water-loving dogs there is access to the River Tone and Norton Brook on the reserve's southern and northern boundaries. The current in these waterways is gentle unless there has been heavy rain. A stand of black poplars is located at the western end of the site, near point 6. The Forestry Commission categorises black poplar as Britain's most endangered native tree due to a lack of suitable habitat and small dispersed populations resulting in difficulties in pollination.

How to get there: Bishop's Hull is at the western edge of the Taunton conurbation and is a short distance north of the A38 on minor roads. The Old Inn is on a sharp bend of Bishop's Hull Road.
Sat Nav TA1 5EG.
Parking: Parking is available in the Old Inn's private car park behind the pub at the landlord's discretion. On-street parking is also available in the village.
OS Map: Explorer 128 Taunton and Blackdown Hills/Landranger 193 Taunton & Lyme Regis. **Grid ref:** ST203246.

THE OLD INN is a down-to-earth pub and B&B in a notably long building formed of three terraced houses dating from the Victorian era. Classic, reasonably-priced pub grub, including a Sunday roast, is served in the bar and lounge areas and there are occasional curry nights, music events (you may even see an Elvis impersonator performing live) and pub quizzes. There is a cosy log burner in the lounge area and a beer garden at the rear. The bar serves one regular real ale. Dogs are welcome in the bar area.
🌐 No website ☎ 01823 617782

Terrain: From the Old Inn you follow suburban streets, mostly on pavements, to Netherclay Community Woodland Nature Reserve. The reserve is flat with a network of well-maintained paths between compartments of densely-planted young woodland. The challenge level is 2, due to a short hill between the village and the reserve.
Challenge level: 2.
Road walking: 0.4 miles/0.6 km.
Livestock: None.
Stiles: None.
Nearest vet: Tone Veterinary Centre, Norton Fitzwarren, TA2 6DG. ☎ 01823 340660.

The Walk

❶ Turn right when exiting the Old Inn and head east along Bishop's Hull Road to a junction next to a church.

❷ Cross the junction and keep going straight ahead on another street (Netherclay). Follow the street downhill as it leaves the village. Here the road narrows and is flanked by walls.

❸ Turn left off the road at a kissing gate and waymarker indicating Netherclay Nature Reserve just after the entrance to Netherclay House residential home. Follow the path for 50 metres and cross a footbridge over the River Tone.

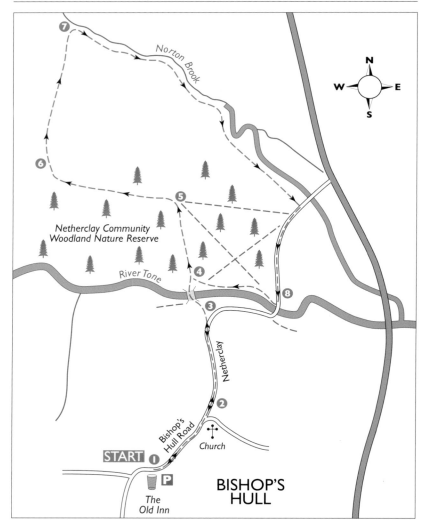

4 At the northern end of the footbridge, when looking directly in front of you, you will see two paths branching slightly to the left and to the right between woodland compartments. Take the path that veers slightly to the left. Continue on this path for 180 metres until you reach another junction of paths.

5 Turn left at the path junction and continue straight ahead for 224 metres, ignoring all paths leading from this straight course and go through a gate. About 40 metres after the gate, go through another gate where two field hedges meet next to a Somerset Wildlife Trust interpretation panel.

6 Turn right after going through the second gate and follow the field edge north for 280 metres until a stream is reached (Norton Brook).

7 Turn right when facing the brook and follow the riverbank for 580 metres to a gate leading out of the reserve onto a minor asphalt road, where you turn right. Follow the road for 200 metres to a gate opposite Mill Cottage.

8 Go through the gate to re-enter the reserve next to the River Tone and continue on the path adjacent to the riverbank, heading upriver until you meet the footbridge you crossed earlier when entering the reserve. From here head back to Bishop's Hull for a refreshing drink at the Old Inn.

9 CROWCOMBE
4.6 miles (7.3 km)

If you and your dog are looking for a good lung and leg workout then this exhilarating walk in the heart of the Quantocks Area of Outstanding Natural Beauty will not disappoint. The views from Hurley Beacon are sublime on a clear day.

The route takes you straight up the steep flank of Hurley Beacon, along a ridge and then back to Crowcombe via Halsway Hill and a path running parallel to the A358: just bear in mind that the weather at the ridge can be several degrees cooler (and windier) than down in the Carew Arms' beer garden, so pack accordingly.

How to get there: Crowcombe is adjacent to the A358 11 miles (17 km) north of Taunton. The Carew Arms is at the eastern end of the main village street.

Sat Nav TA4 4AD for the pub or **TA4 4AA** for the public car park.

Parking: There are a few car-parking spaces at the front of the pub, and a free public car park behind Church House, 300 metres east of the Carew Arms via the main village street.

OS Map: Explorer 140 Quantock Hills & Bridgwater/Landranger 181 Minehead & Brendon Hills. **Grid ref:** ST138367.

> **Terrain:** The route is mostly on well-made paths, although in some places the way is faint due to lack of use. Some of the paths are not waymarked.
> **Challenge level:** 4.
> **Road walking:** 0.7 miles/1.1 km.
> **Livestock:** Possibility of sheep between point 2 and point 10.
> **Stiles:** None.
> **Nearest vet:** Priory Vets, Bishops Lydeard, TA4 3BU.
> ☎ 01823 433361 or White Lodge Vet Clinic, Minehead, TA4 4AT.
> ☎ 01984 634013.

 THE CAREW ARMS, originally known as the Three Lions, has been a public house for over 400 years. Today it is a pub and B&B and still retains its rural charm, with flagstone floors and a woodburner in an inglenook fireplace in the bar area. The bar serves two regular ales, two changing ales and one West Country cider. The food is decent and has received good reviews. There is a large, pleasant beer garden behind the pub with views towards the Brendon Hills. Dogs are allowed in the bar area and beer garden.
⊕ thecarewarms.co.uk
☎ 01984 618631

The Walk

① From the Carew Arms, turn left to head west along the main village street for 310 metres, passing the post office and village shop to reach the thatched Carew Cottage.

② Head uphill on an easily missed (but waymarked) footpath opposite Carew Cottage. The path goes up a few steps from the street and continues uphill between fields.

③ Cross an unmetalled lane and head directly uphill towards mature woodland. Take a few moments to enjoy the grand views of the Brendon Hills to the west.

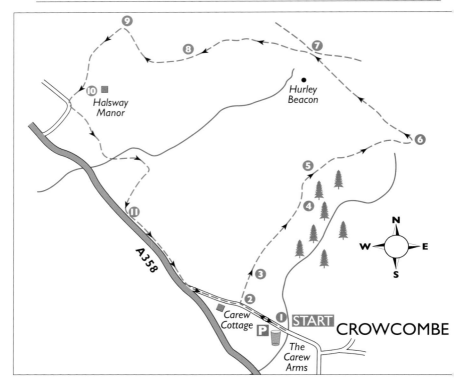

4 Go through a gate at the edge of the woodland and continue uphill with woodland beyond a fence to your right.

5 When reaching the top of the woodland, go through a gate and turn right, angling slightly uphill and away from the woodland, and follow a narrow path to reach a fence which runs more or less along the ridge of the hill.

6 Turn left when meeting the fence and follow it uphill for 800 metres to go through a gate leading onto a wide track. Turn left onto the track to pass the Halsway Post a few metres ahead.

7 Just after Halsway Post is a junction of three paths. Here you bear left to head slightly downhill on the lowest of the paths, which is also the least well-used. Keep to this track and don't head off on any of the tracks leading from it.

8 Fork left at a row of beech trees (an overgrown hedge), heading slightly downhill to follow the row of trees across the hillside.

9 Upon reaching the last tree in the row, turn left 90° to head straight down the hill on the path adjacent to another row of beeches. Continue until reaching a gate leading onto an asphalt yard and a few cottages and farm buildings at Halsway Manor.

10 Turn left after crossing the yard to join a minor road. Continue on the road for 0.7 miles (1.1 km), passing the Quantock School of Riding.

11 Just before reaching the busy A358, turn left onto a path which runs adjacent to the A358, waymarked Quantock Greenways. Continue on this path, passing through a series of gates, until the path meets Crowcombe's main street. Here you join a pavement and head back to the starting point.

10 WEST MONKTON
2.3 miles (3.7 km)

This walk is perfect for a leisurely stroll and includes pleasant rural views, a visit to a churchyard and a tour of a small area of woodland. Your dog will need to be kept on a lead or under close control for most of the route, but it can run free in the woodland between points 5 and 6.

Heading north-east from the Monkton Inn, the route passes a church with a tower dating to the 13th century. If manacles and flagellation interest you, head into the churchyard to view some stocks and a whipping post dating to the 18th century. The church is dedicated to St Augustine (AD 354–430), who was born in Numidia (in present-day north-west Algeria) during the Roman Empire and is considered to be one of Christianity's most important theologians and philosophers.

From the church, the route continues on footpaths and minor roads to a small area of woodland, some of which is dominated by laurel. Natural laurel woodland is nowadays indigenous to just a few tropical and sub-tropical locations around the world but once covered an extensive, contiguous area. The world's remaining native laurel forests are highly valued as they are surviving remnants of the ancient forests of Gondwana.

After forming a circuit through the woodland, the route rejoins the outward route and you retrace your steps back to West Monkton. The village was once within land held by Glastonbury Abbey, lying further to the east. The abbey monks named West Monkton according to its location west of the abbey.

Terrain: The route is mostly on quiet minor roads and footpaths with some views of open countryside, as well as a small area of woodland. There are no steep inclines and the paths are well-maintained.
Challenge level: 2.
Road walking: 0.3 miles/0.5 km.
Livestock: Possibility of cows in a small field between points 5 and 6.
Stiles: 1 with dog board.
Nearest vet: Tone Veterinary Centre, Taunton, TA1 2PD.
☎ 01823 333909.

How to get there: West Monkton is accessed from minor roads 0.9 miles / 1.5 km west of A38 and A361 junction just east of Taunton. The Monkton Inn is on the western side of the village at the junction of Blundell's Lane, Noah's Hill and The Street.
Sat Nav TA2 8NP.
Parking: The Monkton Inn has a large car park, with parking at the landlord's discretion. On-street parking is also available nearby.
OS Map: Explorer 140 Quantock Hills & Bridgwater/Landranger 193 Taunton & Lyme Regis. **Grid ref:** ST260282.

THE PUB

THE MONKTON INN'S owners spent years working in the hospitality industry in South Africa and have brought back some of their favourite dishes. If you've ever fancied trying ostrich, zebra, crocodile babotie or bunny chow (the latter two being amongst South Africa's most popular dishes), this is the place to come. More familiar dishes are also served and the prices are reasonable. The pub has won the *Somerset Gastro Pub of the Year* award

several times and booking ahead is recommended if you want to eat here. The bar serves three real ales and a West Country cider.

Dogs are well catered for with free doggy chews available from the bar and the use of a drinking bowl. Your hairy companion is allowed in the bar area and in the large beer garden.
⊕ themonktoninn.co.uk ☎ 01823 412414

The Walk

. . . .

1 Bear left onto Blundells Lane when exiting the pub car park, then turn right onto The Street at a junction 30 metres ahead. Continue on The Street for

185 metres to a junction with Doster's Lane. Cross Church Hill and continue towards the signposted parish church of St Augustine on a narrow asphalt driveway.

2 At the church, bear left to go up an alley between the graveyard and some houses, and then bear right at the top of the lane. Here you join part of the East Deane Way, a long-distance walking route.

3 After crossing a minor road, go through a gate opposite and continue on a footpath flanked by a laurel hedge and a wall.

4 Turn left after crossing a stile (with a dog board next to it) onto a minor road. Follow the road uphill and turn right when the road swings left, to follow an unmetalled track past a house (Burlinch) and into woodland.

5 When you get to another house (also called Burlinch), turn right to go through a gate into woodland, where you bear left following a right of way marker. Follow the waymarkers as you head uphill,

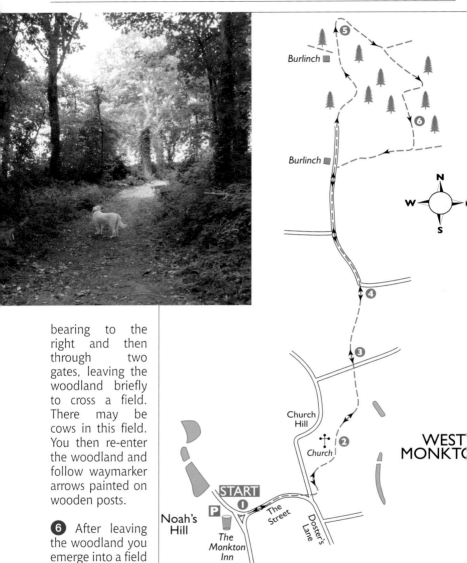

bearing to the right and then through two gates, leaving the woodland briefly to cross a field. There may be cows in this field. You then re-enter the woodland and follow waymarker arrows painted on wooden posts.

6 After leaving the woodland you emerge into a field being overtaken by bracken. Continue straight ahead across the field until you meet a hedge. Here you bear right and follow the hedge until it meets the track just below the first Burlinch cottage you passed earlier. From here, follow the outward route back to West Monkton.

11 CHEW MAGNA
3 miles (4.8 km)

At the heart of this walk is the River Chew, a pretty little waterway that rises near the village of Chewton Mendip, on the high Mendip plateau, before meandering down, eventually joining the Avon on the outskirts of Bristol.

Setting off from the village of Chew Magna, this is a pleasingly higgledy-piggledy route along river banks, down secluded paths and across fields, through one of the loveliest corners of the Chew Valley. You'll cross some ancient stone bridges along the way, and there are plenty of opportunities for your dog to take a dip in the river.

You'll need to put your dog on the lead on a couple of occasions, as there are one or two roads to be navigated here (Chew Magna itself is a bustling little place), but that won't detract from the enjoyment.

How to get there: Chew Magna is 7 miles south of Bristol, on the B3130 road which links the A38 and A37. It can be reached from the south by turning off the A368 at West Harptree.
Sat Nav BS40 8SL.
Parking: There is a free car park behind the Pelican and there are also some parking bays available on the High Street and adjoining side streets.
OS Map: Explorer 154 Bristol West & Portishead/Landranger 182 Weston-super-Mare, Bridgwater & Wells. **Grid ref:** ST576631.

SOMERSET – Dog Friendly Pub Walks

THE PELICAN or 'the Pelly' as it's known locally, is right in the middle of Chew, with a free car park at the rear. Built in the 18th century, it has everything required of a decent village pub - log fires for winter, a sunny terrace for warmer days, a splendid menu and a warm welcome for both you and your dog. The bar has a good selection of wine and serves local beer and cider from Butcombe Brewery.

⊕ butcombe.com/pubs/the-pelican-inn ☎ 01275 331777

The Walk

❶ With the Pelican behind you, turn right. You'll want to keep your dog on the lead for this first bit. After a few paces you'll reach a junction; turn right here and head south on Tunbridge Road. Look out for a church on your right, and a raised pavement to the left, as you make your way down to an old stone bridge over the River Chew. This 15th-century, triple-arched structure contains a curiosity you could easily miss. On the eastern side is a stone trough. This was once used in time of plague, when the village was effectively cut off. Local farmers used to bring food to this bridge and collect their payment from the trough, where coins would be left in sterilising vinegar. After crossing the bridge, carry on straight ahead for about 150 metres, passing the fire station on the right. Just as the road bends to the right, look out for the Coach House on the right. Immediately opposite is a kissing gate leading onto a public footpath through a field.

❷ Once you're through the kissing gate, feel free to take your dog off the lead (providing there's no livestock about). Carry straight on across the field, pass through three gates (two kissing gates, followed by a traditional swing gate). Follow the path straight ahead, keeping the hedge to your left until

Terrain: Some small inclines, but generally flat with clearly marked paths.
Challenge level: 2.
Road walking: 0.5 miles/0.8 km.
Livestock: You may encounter cattle in some of the fields.
Stiles: None.
Nearest vet: Golden Valley Vets, 40a High Street, Chew Magna, BS40 8PW. ☎ 0127 5 331777.

you come to a gate in the bottom left-hand corner of the field. Just after you pass through the gate you'll descend some steep steps. Take care here. At the bottom, turn left and walk across the grass until you reach a bridge. Pass through two gates and over the bridge, at which point you'll emerge into a field. Head across the field to a metal gate. At the gate, pop your dog back on the lead, as you're about to cross a road.

3 Once through the gate, you'll see Chew Court, with a beautiful cricket green to the left and a long tree-lined drive ahead of you. Head down here. After 100 metres or so, the drive will bend to the right. Carry on walking along the gravel path and then follow the path as it bears left. Look ahead, just to the left and you'll see some steps and an opening leading up to the churchyard. Proceed through here and follow the path to the right (almost back on yourself). This will take you down through the churchyard. Exit through a small gate to emerge on North Chew Terrace. Turn left, heading downhill and turn left onto Silver Street. At the end of the road you'll reach a junction, with the mightily impressive Harford House opposite you. Turn right onto Chew Hill.

4 Walk along Chew Hill, with tall stone walls on either side until you come to a bridge over the river. Immediately after the bridge is a small opening leading

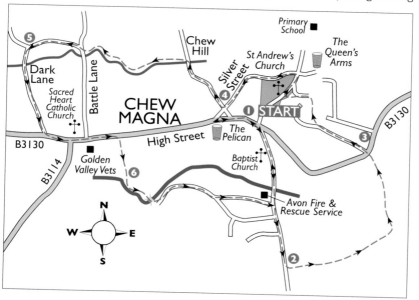

onto a waterside path with grassland to your right. Go through here. Your dog should particularly enjoy this section of the walk as there are lots of opportunities to take a dip in the water. Carry on along the riverside pathway, past a little weir, and through a kissing gate at the bottom left of the field. You'll then emerge onto a narrow pathway, with a wall on your right. At the end of this pathway, you'll emerge onto Battle Lane. It's advisable to put your dog back on the lead here. Turn right at this T-junction and stay on Battle Lane as it veers left. Soon you will come to a fork in the road. Battle Lane continues to the right, but you will take the left fork onto Dark Lane, arriving shortly at a ford.

5 If you're wearing wellies and the water isn't too high, you can probably walk across here. Take care though! Alternatively, you can just head over the footbridge on the left. Your dog will probably opt for a dip in the water. After crossing the ford, continue on Dark Lane, taking care to put your dog back on the lead after 20 metres or so, before reaching the top of the hill. At this point you'll be turning left onto Winford Road, leading onto the High Street. Carry on along here, passing the Catholic church on your left and Golden Valley Vets on your right. After 50 metres, keep an eye out on your right for a gap between cottage No 26 and a row of stone mushrooms to the left. There's an alleyway here - go down it. The path leads back down to the river. Your dog will enjoy more off-lead time here and there's plenty of sniffing about to be done along the path. Continue until you reach the river and walk along it until you come to the bridge.

6 Cross the bridge and continue along the path until you reach another wooden bridge. Once you've crossed it, pop your dog back on the lead for the final stretch. After the bridge you'll emerge on Dumpers Lane. Carry straight on, past Dumpers Farmhouse on your right. When you reach the fork in the road, take the lane on the left (passing a wooden gate on your left). After 100 metres, you'll reach the end of Dumpers Lane. Turn left here, and you'll be back on Tunbridge Road. Head over the stone bridge and back into Chew Magna. The Pelican will be on your left as you rejoin the High Street.

12 WEST HATCH
1.5 miles (2.4 km)

If you enjoy strolling in deciduous woodland this almost-level scenic route is a must. It is perfect for letting your dog run off the lead and your pet will be delighted by the smells and scent trails to follow. The walk is within woodland owned by the Forestry Commission, but you can extend the route by about 0.6 miles (1 km), by continuing through an adjacent nature reserve managed by Somerset Wildlife Trust. Beyond which you will find the settlement of Thurlbear, where you can view a 12th-century Norman church with dramatic gargoyles.

Thurlbear Wood Nature Reserve was once an important resource for hazel coppice and still supports populations of hazel dormice, a rare species that spends most of its life asleep and relies on hazel (usually coppiced) woodland for its survival. Try not to let your dog roam too far from the forestry road within the reserve, as woodland dormice make nests in leaf litter, which may be disturbed by your curious dog.

> **How to get there:** The pub and walk leading from it are at Broadlands Farm, 1.3 miles (2.2 km) south-west of the hamlet of West Hatch. It is a relatively remote area accessed by minor roads leading off the A358 or B3170 heading south from Taunton.
> **Sat Nav TA3 5RS** for the pub or **TA3 5BA** for Thurlbear Wood car park.

SOMERSET – Dog Friendly Pub Walks

Parking: The Farmers Arms has a large car park, with parking at the landlord's discretion. There is also a free public car park at the entrance to Thurlbear Wood at point 2. There is no on-street parking available.
OS Map: Explorer 128 Taunton & Blackdown Hills / Landranger 193 Taunton & Lyme Regis. **Grid ref:** ST272198 for the pub or ST270198 for Thurlbear Wood.

Terrain: The walk begins on a minor public road and heads into Thurlbear Wood on a well-made forestry road. It then briefly enters a field via a footpath before re-joining the woodland on a track leading back to the well-made forestry road. This is an easy walk with very little height variation.
Challenge level: 1.
Road walking: 260 metres.
Livestock: Possibility of cows between points 2 & 3.
Stiles: 1 with space for a dog to pass next to it.
Nearest vet: Kingfisher Veterinary Practice, Taunton, TA1 3BQ.
☎ 01823 327272.

THE FARMERS ARMS inn and B&B is a converted farmhouse dating to the 16th century and retains many original features. In the bar area there are wooden floors, leather sofas, a woodburner and exposed stone walls. There are also two beer gardens which provide good views of the Mendip, Quantock and Brendon hill ranges. Dogs are welcome in all areas of the pub and there is a water bowl and free dog chews available for your four-legged friend. The bar serves four regular real ales (three in winter) and there are regular themed menu days. The food is notably good.
🌐 farmersarmssomerset.co.uk ☎ 01823 480980

The Walk

• •

1 From the entrance to the Farmers Arms, turn right onto the minor road. At the cottages just ahead, bear right again on the signposted road towards Taunton and Slough Green. Continue for 50 metres until meeting a junction of minor roads. Here you bear left and continue for 85 metres to the entrance to Thurlbear Wood.

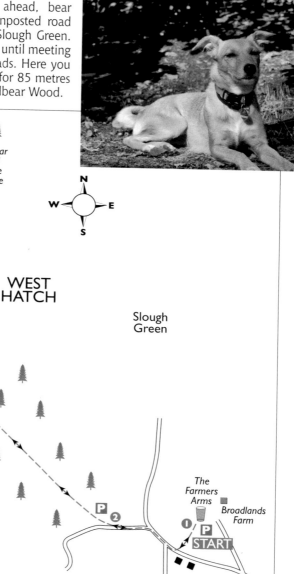

2 Go through a gate leading from Thurlbear Wood car park onto a wide forestry road and continue straight ahead for 440 metres to a public right of way marker indicating a track to the left. Follow this path, heading downhill for 100 metres to a gate.

3 Bear right after going through the gate into the field and follow the fence for 220 metres to cross a small footbridge and go through a stile (with space for a dog to pass next to it) to re-enter the woodland. Here you bear left on a track and continue for 115 metres.

4 Bear right onto a wider track and head uphill to re-join the wide forestry road. You can extend the walk by turning left here by continuing through the pleasant Thurlbear Wood Nature Reserve for 510 metres to the settlement of Thurlbear (turn right at the minor road at Thurlbear; the church is a few metres ahead on your right). Alternatively, turn right and head back to the Farmers Arms on the forestry track, retracing the route you walked earlier.

13 OVER STRATTON
4.8 miles (7.6 km)

This is an enjoyable circuit through tranquil countryside. Nearly half of the route consists of public bridleways, while the remainder traverses fields with some walking on quiet roads. Dogs should be kept on leads or under close control in the fields but can run free on the bridleways which are mostly bounded by hedges. Both dogs and humans will enjoy the variety of terrain, and there are plenty of scent trails with which your canine can indulge its senses.

How to get there: Over Stratton lies just south of the A303, running between Ilminster and Ilchester. The Royal Oak is on the village's main street.
Sat Nav TA13 5LQ.
Parking: There is a car park behind the Royal Oak. Parking is at the landlord's discretion. On-street parking is also available.
OS Map: Explorer 129 Yeovil & Sherborne/Landranger 193 Taunton & Lyme Regis. **Grid ref:** ST434154.

SOMERSET – Dog Friendly Pub Walks

THE ROYAL OAK is a thatched, Grade II listed building with stone walls, an open fire, flagstone floors and solid oak beams which lend it plenty of character. Originally built in the 1600s as a farmhouse, the building was later converted into farm workers' cottages and around the 1850s it became a pub. Many of the buildings in this part of Somerset, including the Royal Oak, are made from beautiful, honey-coloured Hamstone, a Jurassic-era limestone quarried from nearby Ham Hill. In the 19th century there were 200 quarries in operation; now just two remain.

Two regular real ales are served and the menu offers contemporary and classic versions of British pub food. These dishes are supplemented by daily changing specials with an international influence and themed food nights sometimes take place.

The Royal Oak has a well-mannered resident dog that doesn't seem to mind sharing its space and even its water bowl with visiting canines. There are also complimentary doggy chews available. Dogs are permitted anywhere in the pub. There is also a beer garden to laze in during the warmer months.

🌐 royaloakoverstratton.co.uk ☎ 01460 240906

Terrain: The route is through fields and along bridleways on well-waymarked paths with little variation in altitude or gradient.

Challenge level: 1.

Road walking: 0.9 miles/1.4 km.

Livestock: Possibility of sheep and cows between points 2 and 4 and sheep between points 7 and 8.

Stiles: 3, one of which has space for a dog next to it; the other two will require you to lift your dog over them.

Nearest vet: Minster Veterinary Surgery, South Petherton, TA13 5BS.
☎ 01460 241262.

The Walk

① From the Royal Oak turn left and head up the main village street and bear left at the road junction, heading towards Wigborough and Norton sub Hamdon for 0.5 miles (0.8 km), then bear right at the road junction just before the hamlet of Lower Stratton.

② Turn right, going through a gate onto a path next to a monkey puzzle and follow the waymarked path towards Merriot. This is part of the River Parrett Trail, a long-distance walking route. Pass into an adjacent

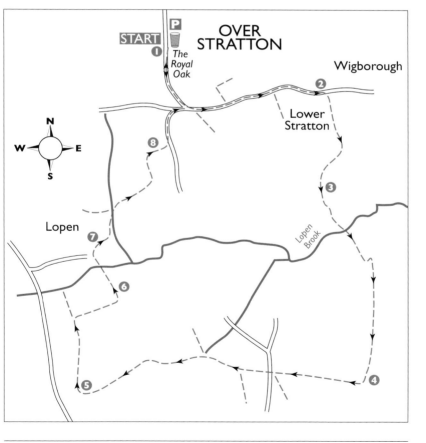

field and follow the trail on a grassy wayleave with crops to your right and hedges and trees to your left. As the field edge curves to the right, go straight ahead onto an easily missed grassy lane flanked by hedges. Shortly after, the path takes you to the edge of another field, with crops to your left and trees to your right. Keep following waymarkers for the River Parrett Trail.

3 Bear left onto a grassy track between two fields with a clump of willows visible ahead. There are no River Parrett Trail waymarkers here. You now go through a series of fields for 0.8 miles (1.3 km) with kissing gates providing access to each field.

4 When meeting a track (Garstone Lane), turn right and continue for 1 mile (1.6 km), crossing a minor road and heading towards Lopen, indicated by a public bridleway waymarker.

5 At a bridleway T-junction, turn right onto a grassy track which may be a bit overgrown. Continue on this track for 440 metres until meeting a metal field gate. Here you turn right (without going through the gate) to continue for 260 metres on a wide, grassy track bounded by hedges.

6 Cross a stile (with space for a dog to pass next to it) in the hedge to your left, following the right of way marker and passing a yard and some industrial buildings at Lopen. Cross a small bridge and bear left onto an asphalt road, going over a speedbump into Lopen Business Park.

7 Just after passing the gates of the business park, bear right next to a stone house, going through a high metal gate into a field containing a long agricultural building. Here you bear left to pass between the left-hand side of the building and a hedge. Just past a couple of silos at the end of the building, turn left into an orchard and follow the hedge on your right. At the corner of the orchard, cross two stiles (no dog boards or spaces for dog access) into another orchard. Cut across the orchard, bearing slightly left towards a couple of green water tanks next to a small field.

8 Go through a gate next to the water tanks onto a farm track. At the end of the track, bear left onto a minor asphalt road heading into Over Stratton. Follow the road as it swings to the right, then turn left (signposted for South Petherton) onto the main village street, to head back to the Royal Oak.

14 MONTACUTE
1.3 miles (2.1 km)

This short walk culminates with expansive views from the top of a folly, ascended via a spiral stairway. Indy the dog managed it too, not wanting to be left behind at the base of the tower.

The village's name is derived from *Mons Acutus*, the Roman name for the conical Saint Michael's Hill just west of the village. After leaving Montacute the route heads up this hill through a steep field which may contain cows. The hill is adorned with woodland and topped with Saint Michael's Tower, built as a folly in 1760 for Montacute House. After admiring the panoramic views from the hill, you head back to Montacute.

The hill has an illustrious history: In 1030 Tolfig, a local blacksmith, started digging on the hillside, having apparently had a series of dreams telling him to do so. He dug up a black flint cross that was taken to Waltham Abbey, which consequently became a site of pilgrimage. The cross was later taken to Scotland by the last Anglo-Saxon monarch, Queen (later Saint) Margaret, when she fled the Norman Conquest of England. The cross was named the Holy Ruid, which gave its name to Holyrood in Edinburgh. The cross was seized by the English in the 14th century and was taken to Durham Cathedral. It is now lost, presumably having been destroyed in the English Reformation in the 16th century.

Terrain: From Montacute, the route leads through a field with no distinct path and enters a small woodland on Saint Michael's Hill on a wide, well-made path. The return journey skirts the edge of this woodland and heads back through the field. The walk is short but steep.

Challenge level: 3.

Road walking: None.

Livestock: Possibility of cattle before point 3.

Stiles: None.

Nearest vet: Isle Valley Vets, Stoke sub Hamdon, TA14 6QE.
☎ 01935 310930.

How to get there: Montacute is just a few miles west of Yeovil and is easily accessed from the A3088 just to the north of the village. The King's Arms Inn is on a bend at the junction of Middle Street and Bishopston.

Sat Nav TA15 6UU.

Parking: The King's Arms Inn has a car park next to the pub. Parking is at the landlord's discretion. On-street parking is also available.

OS Map: Explorer 129 Yeovil & Sherborne / Landranger 183 Yeovil & Frome / Landranger 193 Taunton & Lyme Regis.

Grid ref: ST496170.

THE PUB
THE KINGS ARMS INN dates back to the 17th century, when it was a coaching inn. The inn, as well as many other buildings in the village, is constructed with Hamstone quarried from nearby Ham Hill, endowing it with an attractive honey colour. The bar area contains several comfy sofas and there are two restaurant areas. There is also a beer garden behind the pub. Dogs are permitted in the bar area and beer garden. The bar serves three regular ales and one West Country cider.

🌐 thekingsarmsinn.co.uk
☎ 01935 822255

The Walk

● ●

1 Leaving the Kings Arms Inn, turn right to head up the lane next to a church and turn right at the regal Abbey Farm, a Grade I listed building dating to the

16th century. From there, go through two gates and follow the waymarker for Hedgecock Hill Wood. This is part of the Monarch's Way, a long-distance footpath that approximates the escape route of King Charles II after his defeat at the battle of Worcester in 1651. However, the section of the route between Montacute and Hamdon Hill, 1.2 miles (2 km) to the west, is ancient and has pre-Roman origins.

2 Ignore a waymarker indicating a right of way to the right heading uphill

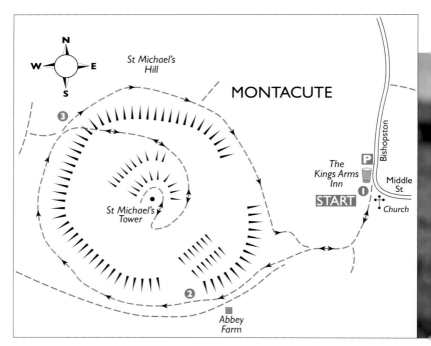

through woodland, where there is no dog access over a stile, and keep going directly ahead, passing under some powerlines and skirting the contour of the hill, keeping the woodland to your right. At the western side of the woodland you will find a gate.

❸ Go through the gate and continue straight uphill on a wide track, until you reach Saint Michael's Tower at the top of the hill. The expansive views from here are worth savouring, but it's recommended that you ascend the spiral stairway of the tower not only because it's fun, but also because the panoramic views are splendid.

After enjoying the vistas, head back through the woodland to the field. For the sake of variation, instead of heading back the way you came, head to the right when entering the field, to skirt the woodland edge, keeping the woodland to your right and walking downhill to join the route just above Abbey Farm. From here you retrace your footsteps back to The Kings Arms.

15 KNOWLE
3.6 miles (5.8 km)

This linear but enjoyable walk in the Somerset Levels takes you along part of King's Sedgemoor Drain, where you might see swans, as well as kingfishers if you are lucky, and other water-dwelling birds. Most of the Levels are not conducive to dog walking due to the lack of maintained footpaths, livestock (usually cows) in the fields and stiles that are not dog–friendly. However, this pleasant amble is livestock-free from halfway between points 2 and 3 (although there were none when I visited), and the waterway is a peaceful place where fishermen contentedly cast their lines. King's Sedgemoor Drain is well stocked and has hosted the National Fishing Championships. It is also important for eels, which make the long return journey to the Sargasso Sea (off the North American seaboard) on an annual migration.

The 10.5-mile King's Sedgemoor Drain was constructed in 1795 to make the peaty and waterlogged area suitable for grazing by creating a gravity-fed drain into the River Parrett (most other drains in the region rely on pumps). At the time of the drain's construction locals were concerned that they would lose their commoners' rights to the surrounding land. Their fears were confirmed shortly after the land was drained.

Your dog will enjoy the many scent trails on this walk and can be let off the leash from halfway between points 2 and 3; however, water-loving dogs should be kept out of the water when near fishermen as a matter of courtesy. Despite the drainage, the area remains important habitat for wading birds.

This walk can be extended by continuing along King's Sedgemoor Drain past Parchey Bridge. As an alternative, this walk could be started from the other end by leaving your car at the free public car park at Parchey Bridge, 0.82 miles (1.3 km) east of Chedzoy, walking to the Knowle Inn and then returning to your car.

Terrain: After a short distance across some fields and on grassy tracks, the route follows a flat asphalt path along King's Sedgemoor Drain.
Challenge level: 1.
Road walking: None.
Livestock: Possibly until halfway between points 2 and 3.
Stiles: 3, two are easily bypassed by a dog but you will have to lift your dog over the third.
Nearest vet: Orchard Vets, Glastonbury, BA6 9XE. ☎ 01458 832972.

How to get there: Knowle is a small hamlet, with a pub and a couple of houses just west of Cossington. It is on the A39, 1.6 miles / 2.6 km east of Junction 23 of the M5 motorway.
Sat Nav TA7 8PN for the pub or **TA7 8RW** for Parchey Bridge car park.
Parking: There is a car park behind the Knowle Inn, with parking at the landlord's discretion. Access is via a minor road on the western side of the pub. There is also a free public car park at Parchey Bridge.
OS Map: Explorer 140 Quantock Hills & Bridgwater/Landranger 182 Weston-super-Mare. **Grid ref:** ST335399 for the pub ST352377 for the public car park at Parchey Bridge.

THE KNOWLE INN dates from the 16th century when it was the only licensed public house in the parish and was a coaching inn for many years. Its beer garden has won awards for its floral displays and a commendation by the *Telegraph*. The bar serves two regular ales and one West Country cider. Meals are reasonably priced and the menu includes some pub classics as well as specials. Dogs are permitted in the bar and beer garden.
⊕ theknowleinn.co.uk ☎ 01278 683330

The Walk

. . . .

1 From the Knowle Inn, cross the busy A39 to an agricultural building diagonally opposite the pub. Follow the right of way marker through a yard next to the building and through a gate into a field. Cross the field bearing left, to head under some power lines towards a gate.

2 Go through the gate

and over the stile opposite (there is a dog board next to the stile) and cross the field bearing to the left to go over another stile. There is no dog board here; however, all but the largest dogs should fit under the fence next to the stile. Continue on the grassy track, crossing another stile with space next to it for a dog to pass.

3 Turn right just after another stile – you will have to lift your dog over this one – to go over a footbridge spanning King's Sedgemoor Drain. After crossing the bridge turn left to go through a gate. Continue on this waterside route, crossing a minor road at Bradney Bridge, just south of Bawdrip.

4 The end of this walk is at Parchey Bridge, just east of Chedzoy. From here you can return to the Knowle Inn or continue your walk along King's Sedgemoor Drain if you fancy extending the route.

16 BABCARY
2.1 miles (3.4 km)

Part of this pleasant route is through Babcary Meadows Nature Reserve, a 13.6-hectare site managed for its unimproved grassland rich in herbaceous species. The reserve conserves the last traditionally-managed meadows in south Somerset and is one of the few remaining in England. From March until the hay is cut around mid-July, a myriad of plant species imbues the fields with a variety of hues, creating a gorgeous palette. The reserve is also important habitat for a variety of birds, insects and mammals.

Leaving the reserve on part of the Macmillan Way West, a long-distance footpath, the route continues along a track bounded by hedges and then heads through fields to join a minor road heading back to Babcary. Well-behaved dogs can run leash-free in the reserve if there are no cows present, and in the lanes between points 4 and 5.

How to get there: Babcary is 0.6 miles (1 km) east of the A37, 5 miles (8 km) north of Ilchester and 2 miles south of Lydford-on-Fosse. The Red Lion Inn is on a T-Junction at the eastern end of Main Street. **Sat Nav TA11 7ED**.
Parking: The pub has a large car park with parking at the landlord's discretion. On-street parking is available nearby.
OS Map: Explorer 129 Yeovil and Sherborne/Landranger 183 Yeovil & Frome. **Grid ref:** ST564286.

THE RED LION INN is a thatched building with a large, attractive beer garden, elegant dining room and two bar areas. The inn has been tastefully modernised and the exposed oak beams, flagstone floors, woodburner and open fire lend it a timeless ambience. The meals are good-quality and the menu includes homemade pizzas from a wood-fired oven. The bar serves three regular and two changing ales, and one West Country cider. Dogs are welcome in the bar areas and in the garden.

⊕ redlionbabcary.co.uk ☎ 01458 223230

Terrain: The section through Babcary Meadows Nature Reserve may be indistinct in places after harvest, and waymarking is lacking within the reserve. However, the route is fairly well-used and a faint path is visible through the meadows. After joining an unmetalled lane (Lydford Lane), the route is obvious. The entire walk is flat.
Challenge level: 1.
Road walking: 664 metres.
Livestock: Possibility of cows between points 2 and 4, and 5 and 6.
Stiles: None.
Nearest vet: Kingfisher Veterinary Practice, Taunton, TA1 3BQ.

The Walk

● ●

1 Leaving the Red Lion Inn, turn right and head along North Street (a quiet, dead-end lane), for 500 metres, ignoring a road leading off to your right, and passing some quaint cottages. North Street becomes an unmetalled lane just beyond the cottages. Turn right at a ford, then left after 40 metres, to cross a small footbridge over a stream and enter Babcary Meadows Nature Reserve.

2 Angle slightly to the right when crossing the field to a large gap in the hedge about 100 metres in front of you. After going through the gap, angle slightly to the left and continue on the faint track towards a gap in a hedge at the north-eastern corner of the field. Go through the gap and follow the hedge east for 117 metres, going through a gate into another field. Continue directly

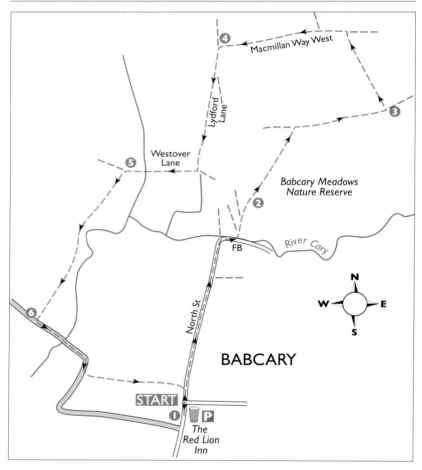

ahead on the same course across the field. This is the fourth field you have passed through since leaving the footbridge.

3 Turn left to head north when you meet the hedge, following the hedge and keeping it to your right. After passing through a gap in the hedge in the field corner directly in front of you, turn left and follow the path. This is part of the Macmillan Way West.

4 Turn left when you meet an unmetalled lane (Lydford Lane). After 330 metres you come to a junction of tracks; here you turn right onto the track that is obviously more frequently used (Westover Lane). Follow this for 180 metres until an easily missed kissing gate in the hedge on your left. The kissing gate is almost opposite a more visible metal gate on

your right-hand side. There is a waymarker next to the kissing gate.

5 Go through the kissing gate into a field with a hedge to your left. Follow the hedge south and when the hedge ends, continue on the same course towards a gate in the hedge directly in front of you across the field.

6 Go through the gate onto a minor road and turn left towards Babcary. When the road swings to the right at the village school, bear left onto a footpath. A waymarker here indicates North Street. Continue on this path, going through a kissing gate and passing a tennis court and playpark. When you meet North Street, turn right and continue for 110 metres to the Red Lion Inn.

17 WOOKEY HOLE & EBBOR GORGE
2.6 miles (4.2 km)

If you fancy a workout coupled with some great views, this walk hits the mark. The route takes you and your dog steeply up into the Mendip Hills and down again through the stunning Ebbor Gorge National Nature Reserve. The views are worth the effort, with Glastonbury Tor rising from the flatlands stretching out to the west. After Ebbor Gorge the path levels out and you return to Wookey Hole via a couple of fields and a short stretch on a minor road.

A less exertive alternative to this circuit, but which includes a visit to the unmissable Ebbor Gorge, would be to follow the route in reverse to point 5, where you continue straight ahead or turn left (ignoring the path leading uphill to your right) on well-made and relatively flat paths leading into Ebbor Woods at the foot of the Gorge. Well-controlled dogs can run free in the gorge and in woodland between points 4 and 6, and points 2 and 4 if no sheep are present.

The cave complex at Wookey Hole is a tourist attraction that draws thousands of tourists every year. The caves have been used by animals for at least 50,000 years and the remains of rhinoceros, bear, mammoth, hyaena and lion have been found during excavations. Celtic tribes used one of the caves as a burial chamber and the remains of Roman lead mines have also been discovered nearby. The River Axe begins in the catchment above the caves (and empties into the Bristol Channel near Brean Down: see Walk 20). Deep within the caves, explorers have seen the Axe thundering down a passage 12 metres high by 1.5 metres wide, which has been described as a magnificent sight.

SOMERSET – Dog Friendly Pub Walks

How to get there: Wookey Hole is 1.7 miles (2.8 km) north of Wells and can be accessed via a minor road leading off the A371. The Wookey Hole Inn is located on the High Street.

Sat Nav BA5 1BP for the pub or **BA5 1BE** for the public car park

Parking: There is a small car park 80 metres north of the Wookey Hole Inn, opposite a church. Parking is at the landlord's discretion. There is also a pay-and-display car park on the west side of the River Axe opposite the pub.

OS Map: Explorer 141 Cheddar Gorge & Mendip Hills West/Landranger 182 Weston-super-Mare. **Grid ref:** ST532475 for the pub or ST531475 for the public car park.

Terrain: The section from Wookey Hole to the edge of the plateau is through steep fields. The section heading downhill from the plateau through Ebbor Gorge is on well-made paths through ancient woodland. Some of the downhill sections are steep, but there are steps and it's unlikely you'll slip.

Challenge level: 4.

Road walking: 580 metres.

Livestock: Possibility of sheep from point 2 until entering woodland after point 3.

Stiles: 4 with dog boards.

Nearest vet: Axe Valley Vets, Wells, BA5 2AW. ☎ 01749 670966.

THE PUB

THE WOOKEY HOLE INN has a traditional exterior that belies a uniquely decorated gastropub. The décor is a fusion of laid-back Glastonbury and urban chic. There is a large, pleasant beer garden and the bar serves three changing ales (two in winter) and a West Country cider. The food is good quality and it's necessary to book ahead if you plan on eating here at weekends. Dogs are allowed in the bar area and beer garden.

⊕ wookeyholeinn.com ☎ 01749 676677

The Walk

1 From the Wookey Hole Inn, turn right to head north up the High Street for 150 metres, then turn right up School Hill. Wookey Hole Fun Park and a former papermill (closed in 2008) is visible on your left as you gain height.

2 Go through a gate on your left just before School Hill swings 45° to the right. The path is waymarked as the Monarch's Way, a 615-mile route that approximates the escape of King Charles II of England in 1651 after the Battle

of Worcester, the final battle of the English Civil War. Follow the path as it heads uphill past a deer enclosure and cross a stile (with a dog board next to it) to continue up the steep path into a narrow field. Go straight ahead over another stile (with adjacent dog board) and continue directly uphill on a faint path through three fields. Glastonbury Tor is visible rising from the plain behind you.

❸ At the top of the hill, turn left when

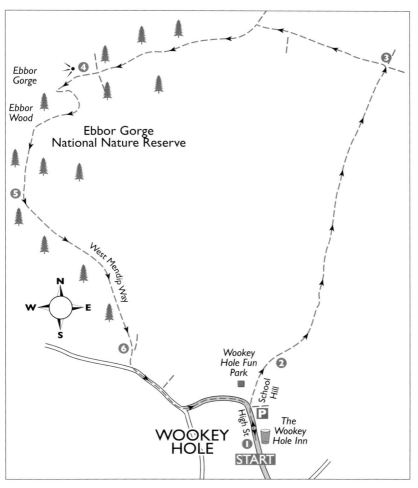

you meet a drystone wall. Follow the wall, which becomes a fence, for 300 metres before going over a stile (with a dog board next to it) into another field. When meeting a metal gate and water trough, turn left to head downhill (don't go through the gate), following the fence. Then go through a gate into Ebbor Gorge on the path marked as the West Mendip Way.

4 After viewing the top of Ebbor Gorge from the impressive viewpoint, head downhill through woodland on the sometimes steep but stepped path.

5 At a path T-junction at the bottom of the hill, turn left and continue on the West Mendip Way which leads out of the woodland and through a couple of fields to meet a road just outside Wookey Hole village. Alternatively, you could turn right at point 5 to head into Ebbor Gorge National Nature Reserve. This

detour is made enjoyable by pleasant deciduous woodland and interesting rock formations within the gorge.

6 Turn left onto the minor road and continue to the High Street, ignoring Titlands Lane which branches off to the right just before you enter Wookey Hole village. Turn right when meeting the High Street to return to the Wookey Hole Inn.

18 GLASTONBURY
2.5 miles (4.1 km)

This trip to the iconic tor at Glastonbury takes you along pavements, public footpaths and a short stretch on a quiet minor road. The final ascent to the tor is steep, but the panoramic views over the expansive Somerset levels are the reward. Although this walk can be busy during holiday times, it is still suitable for dogs, which can run free but under close control between points 2 and 3 and on the grassy area surrounding the tor.

Glastonbury was once the destination of one of the most important medieval pilgrimage routes in Western Christendom (the others being to Rome, Jerusalem and Santiago de Compostela). More recently, the town has become a locus of New Age and Neopagan enthusiasts, evidenced by the plethora of esoteric shops on the High Street. Shopping here is a unique cultural experience and you may be served by someone dressed as a wizard or a fairy.

Glastonbury Tor rises starkly above the Somerset Levels and was once known as the Isle of Avalon. Prior to drainage in medieval times the tor was indeed an island in a landscape of shallow lakes and marshy plains. The earliest written reference to the tor is a 13th-century text describing Saint Patrick's return to Ireland in the 5th century, when he apparently discovered an ancient ruined oratory on the tor's summit and became leader of a group of hermit monks. Excavations on the tor in 1964-66 revealed the remains of monks' cells dating to the 6th century. The tor is topped with a tower dedicated to Saint Michael, who is mentioned in the Bible, Torah and Quran and as such, is venerated by Christians, Jews and Muslims.

Terrain: The route out of Glastonbury is on pavements and a quiet lane, then on a steep, well-made footpath through a parkland landscape to a flat stretch of 330 metres on a quiet lane. From there you ascend to the summit of Glastonbury Tor on a well-made path. The final 200 metres to the tor's summit are steep.
Challenge level: 3.
Road walking: 0.5 miles/0.8 km (560 metres of which are along pavements).
Livestock: Possibility of sheep between points 2 and 3 and around the tor.
Stiles: None.
Nearest vet: Orchard Vets, Glastonbury, BA6 9XE. ☎ 01458 832972.

How to get there: Glastonbury lies south of Wells at the junction of the A39 and A361. The George & Pilgrims is at the bottom (i.e. the western end) of the High Street.
Sat Nav BA6 9DP.
Parking: There is a pay-and-display car park at St John's Square behind the George & Pilgrims. On-street parking is limited.
OS Map: Explorer 141 Cheddar Gorge & Mendip Hills West/Landranger 183 Yeovil & Frome, 182 Weston-super-Mare. **Grid ref:** ST498389.

THE GEORGE & PILGRIMS HOTEL is Grade I listed and is the oldest purpose-built pub in South West England, dating from 1475. It was originally constructed as accommodation for pilgrims visiting Glastonbury Abbey and by the mid-19th century it was known as the George Hotel; its current name preserves both its former names. After the Dissolution of the Monasteries in the late 1530s, the building was owned by the Duke of Somerset, the brother-in-law of King Henry VIII of England (1491–1547) but was neglected and fell into disrepair. In 1658 the building was divided and a horse-powered malt mill was installed. The hotel still retains some original features and its historic value makes it worth a visit. Apparently, it is one of the most haunted hotels in Britain.
The bar serves three changing ales and two regular ales, and one West Country cider. Dogs are allowed in the seating areas in the alcoves to the right of the main doorway as you enter.
⊕ historicinnz.co.uk/glastonbury
☎ 01458 831146

The Walk

1 From the George & Pilgrims head uphill on the High Street. It's worth loitering here to window-shop before continuing on your way. At the top of the High Street, turn right onto Lambrook Street and follow the waymarkers for Glastonbury Tor.

2 Turn left to continue uphill on Dod Lane, going through the gate at the end of the lane, where you leave the village and follow the path uphill in a parkland landscape. There may be some sheep grazing here.

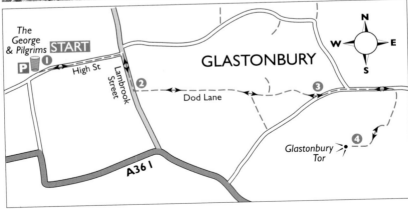

3 When you meet a minor public road (Wellhouse Lane), turn left and continue for 330 metres, then go through a gate onto an asphalt path heading towards the tor, which is visible ahead. Well-controlled dogs can run free here without a leash. Continue on this path until you reach the top of the tor. The final few metres below the summit are steep, but the panoramic views across the Somerset Levels are fantastic.

19 CHEDDAR GORGE
2.8 miles (4.5 km)

The majestic Cheddar Gorge is one of Somerset's most visited attractions and this excursion along the top of its southern cliff is one of Somerset's finest walks. After leaving the cosy White Hart you ascend the steep Jacob's Ladder and continue uphill, heading east above the deep gash of the gorge, accompanied by great views. As the ground levels out, you join the West Mendip Way and head downhill through Bubwith Acres Nature Reserve to the outskirts of Cheddar, before briefly heading uphill to rejoin the route near the top of Jacob's Ladder, where you can ascend a lookout tower for some fantastic views. You then descend the Ladder to return to the starting point. There is an entrance fee charged to access Jacob's Ladder, which is owned by the Longleat Estate. Jacob's Ladder is grandly named after the celestial stairway connecting earth with heaven, dreamed by Jacob in the Book of Genesis. Unlike the biblical ladder, the steps up Cheddar Gorge include rest stops with benches.

The 9,000-year-old remains of Cheddar Man, Britain's oldest intact skeleton were found in Cheddar Gorge in 1903. However, incomplete skeletal remains dating back 12,000 years have also been found in the Gorge.

If you or your dog don't fancy tackling the steep steps of Jacob's Ladder, you could start the walk at Point 5 (and avoid the entrance fee to the southern cliff of the gorge). Well-controlled dogs can be let off the leash anywhere after point 2. The few hundred metres above Jacob's Ladder can be busy in summer. However, Bubwith Acres Nature Reserve, home to some rare grassland plant species, is infrequently visited and you will most likely have at least half the route to yourself.

Terrain: This walk heads up steep concrete steps on Jacob's Ladder before continuing steeply uphill adjacent to Cheddar Gorge on a wide, eroded path. It then descends through Bubwith Acres Nature Reserve on well-made paths before joining an unmetalled lane. At the outskirts of Cheddar, you join a narrow, but well-made path to the top of Jacob's Ladder, which you descend to return to the White Hart.
Challenge level: 4.
Road walking: 230 metres along pavements.
Livestock: None.
Stiles: None.
Nearest vet: Alexandra and Hillyfields Vets, Winscombe, BS25 1AE. ☎ 01934 843381.

How to get there: Cheddar is just off the A371, 8 miles (12.4 km) north of Wells. The White Hart is located in The Bays, just off the main road running through the gorge.
Sat Nav BS27 3QN.
Parking: There is a car park behind the White Hart, with parking at the landlord's discretion. On-street parking nearby is limited, especially during the summer months.
OS Map: Explorer 141 Cheddar Gorge & Mendip Hills West/Landranger 182 Weston-super-Mare. **Grid ref:** ST462538.

THE PUB

THE WHITE HART is a cosy, down-to-earth traditional pub located in a quiet suburban area away from the tourist hordes. There is a small beer garden to the side of the pub and benches out the front. In the colder months there is an open fire to enjoy. Two regular ales and one changing ale are served and the meals are reasonably priced; the popular Sunday roast is particularly good value. Dogs are welcome in any area of the pub and in the beer garden.
⊕ thewhitehartcheddar.co.uk ☎ 01934 741261

The Walk

· ·

❶ Head down a narrow street more or less opposite the White Hart and cross a footbridge over a stream (Cheddar Yeo) to join the main road running through the gorge (B3135). Here you turn left to head uphill on the pavement, then cross the road to enter a building advertising entry to Jacob's Ladder and lookout tower. Having paid your entry fee, follow the path up the steep flight of steps.

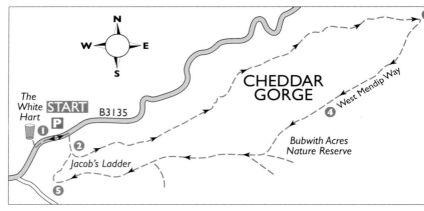

2 At the top of the steps you can ascend the lookout tower just to your right – or save that treat for the end of the walk. Pass through a gate to the left of Jacob's Ladder to head uphill on a wide track, where some interpretation panels provide information on the geology, history and wildlife associated with the gorge. The path is steep, but there are great views of the gorge and the Somerset Levels to the west, and the distinct cone of Glastonbury Tor is clearly visible. Ignore a stile and gate in a fence on your right and keep following the fence uphill. Here, near the top of the gorge, the walk levels out and you pass through a gate into a small area of broadleaf woodland.

3 Turn right at a waymarker next to a birch, indicating the West Mendip Way, and cross an unmetalled track after 200 metres to continue straight ahead to a gate. You may have to vault this (it may be padlocked), but your dog should fit underneath. After the gate the route heads downhill.

4 Go through another gate into Bubwith Acres Nature Reserve. Continue downhill through the reserve for 360 metres and exit via another gate. Keep following the track; the West Mendip Way bears to the left but you continue straight ahead downhill.

5 Join an asphalt lane and immediately bear right, almost doubling back on yourself. You then bear left onto a footpath to head uphill behind some houses. After 140 metres you will arrive at the top of Jacob's Ladder. From here you descend to the White Hart.

20 BREAN
5.2 miles (8.3 km)

You can fill your lungs with wholesome sea air on this seaside jaunt which takes you along Brean beach and up to a circuit of Brean Down before returning back to the Brean Down Inn along the beach. Dogs are allowed on the beach all year and they will undoubtedly enjoy charging around on the sands. Without doubt, I got the impression that this was Indy's favourite walk in Somerset.

Brean Down is a nature reserve and Site of Special Scientific Interest owned by the National Trust and is a promontory 97 metres high extending 1.5 miles (2 km) into the Bristol Channel. For millennia the site was of major strategic importance and guarded the entrance to the Bristol Channel since at least the early Bronze Age (around 2,500 BC). Excavations have also revealed the remains of a Roman temple dating from around the 4th century and several Roman coins have also been found. The fort at the western end of Brean Down was built in 1865 to protect sea access to Bristol and Cardiff and was rearmed with anti-aircraft guns at the beginning of the Second World War.

How to get there: Brean is about 6 miles (9.4 km) north of Burnham-on-Sea and can be accessed from minor roads leading off the A370. The Brean Down Inn is next to Warren Farm Holiday Park.
Sat Nav TA8 2RR.
Parking: There is a car park at the Brean Down Inn, with no on-street parking available. Pay-and-display car parks are available at the northern end of Brean beach, and there is an option of parking on the beach (above the high-tide line!) opposite Brean Farm, about 700 metres north of the Brean Down Inn, at a good price.
OS Map: Explorer 153 Weston-super-Mare & Bleadon Hill/Landranger 182 Weston-super-Mare. **Grid ref:** ST297569. or ST296585 for the public car park.

Terrain: The section from the Brean Down Inn along the beach for 1 mile (1.6 km) is flat. However, the steps up to Brean Down are impressively steep. An alternative route to the summit is to follow the road and path between points 2 and 4. The road is flat and the path has a relatively gentle gradient. Once you are at the top of Brean Down the path undulates but is without steep gradients.
Challenge level: 3.
Road walking: None.
Livestock: None.
Stiles: None.
Nearest vet: Blake Vets, Burnham-on-Sea, TA8 2ET.
☎ 01278 794794.

THE BREAN DOWN INN serves the surrounding holiday parks and can be busy in the evening during the summer. It has a large, covered outdoor seating area, as well as a conservatory area and bar/restaurant, in which there is a woodburner to enjoy on cooler days. The pub exudes a cheerful holiday atmosphere and serves classic pub grub as well as some bespoke items, all at a good price. There is one regular ale, one changing ale, and two regular ciders. Dogs are permitted anywhere in the bar and restaurant areas. Closed October to March (inclusive).

⊕ No website ☎ 01278 751420

The Walk

. . . .

❶ From the Brean Down Inn, turn left to head south for 60 metres. At the brick building (Looe Cottage), cross the road to a sandy track opposite, which leads to the beach. Turn right when facing the sea and head north for 1 mile (1.6 km) to the slipway below Brean Down Cove Café.

The site of an Iron Age settlement that was later an Anglo-Saxon burial ground is at the base of Brean Down, 215 metres north of the slipway.

2 Go up the slipway to Brean Down Cove Café (public toilets are available outside the café) and continue on the asphalt track behind the café, to head up the steep steps leading up to Brean

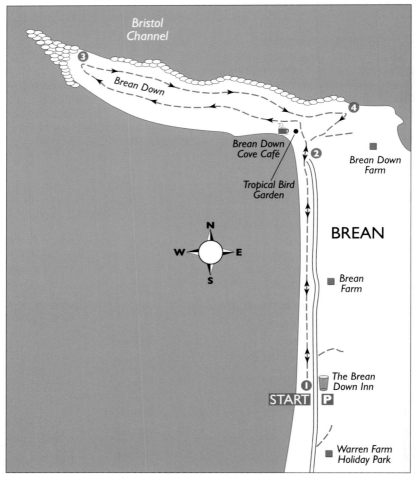

Down. Here you may hear the screeching of exotic birds from the adjacent Tropical Bird Garden.

If you'd rather take an easier route up the hill, head from point 2 to point 4 via the asphalt road adjacent to the car park, which leads to Brean Down Farm, then bear left to head uphill on an asphalt track. Once at the top of Brean Down, bear left (west) to follow the path to the old fort at the western end of the promontory.

❸ After exploring the old fort and enjoying the views, continue on the path on the northern side of the promontory with views towards Weston-super-Mare, until you meet an asphalt path at the eastern end of Brean Down.

❹ Head downhill on the asphalt path to join a flat asphalt track at the bottom of the hill. Here you turn right to head back to Brean Down Cove Café and retrace your route back to the start.

A SELECTION OF OTHER DOG FRIENDLY PUBS IN SOMERSET

© Lorna Anness

AXBRIDGE – The Crown
BRADFORD-ON-TONE – The White Horse
BURROWBRIDGE – The King Alfred Inn
BURTLE – The Duck
CATCOTT – The Crown Inn, The King William Inne
CHARD – Candlelight Inn
CHEDDAR – The Bath Arms, The Riverside Inn
CHIDEOCK – George Inn
CONGRESBURY – The White Hart
COSSINGTON – The Red Tile Inn
EAST LAMBROOK – Rose & Crown
EAST LYNG – The Rose & Crown
EXFORD – Exmoor White Horse Inn
FIVEHEAD – The Crown Inn

GODNEY – The Sheppey
HINTON ST GEORGE – Dinnington Docks
ILMINSTER – The Dolphin, The George
KILVE – The Hood Arms
KINGSDON – The Kingsdon Inn,
LOWER ODCOMBE – The Masons Arms
LYDFORD-ON-FOSSE – The Cross Keys Inn
MINEHEAD – The Hairy Dog
MONKSILVER – Notley Arms
MOORLAND – Thatchers Arms
NORTH PETHERTON – The Globe Inn
NORTON FITZWARREN – The Allerford Inn
NORTON SUB HAMDON – The Lord Nelson
PITNEY – Halfway House
PORLOCK – The Ship Inn
PURITON – The Puriton Inn
SOMERTON – The White Hart
SOUTH PETHERTON – The Brewers Arms
STOKE SUB HAMDON – Fleur de Lis, The Cat Head Inn
TAUNTON – The Plough Inn
THORNBURY – The Swan
WELLS – The City Arms, The Globe Inn
WEST CHINNOCK – The Muddled Man
WEST HUNTSPILL – The Crossways Inn
WESTHAY – The Bird in Hand,
WINCANTON – The Nog Inn
WINSCOMBE – The Penscot Inn
WORTH – The Pheasant Inn